AMERICO MICHAEL

SURROUNDED BY ANGELS

A Journey in Transformation

Heavenly Messengers

AUTHORHOUSE™
1663 LIBERTY DRIVE, SUITE 200
BLOOMINGTON, IN 47403
WWW.AUTHORHOUSE.COM
PHONE: 1-800-839-8640

authorHOUSE®

FIRST PUBLISHED BY AUTHORHOUSE 01/17/2008

ISBN: 978-1-4343-5004-6 (SC)

COVER DESIGN AND BOOK LAYOUT BY M. PALMER DESIGN
WWW.MPALMERDESIGN.COM

ANGEL ARTWORK © 2006 MIKKI CULLY STUDIOS
WWW.MIKKICULLYSTUDIOS.COM

ANGEL LOGO BY TGR COMMUNICATIONS

RESOURCES:
WWW.HEAVENLYMESSENGERS.NET
WWW.HEALTHYLIVINGGUIDE.COM
WWW.GEMINESS.COM

PRINTED IN THE UNITED STATES OF AMERICA
BLOOMINGTON, INDIANA

THIS BOOK IS PRINTED ON ACID-FREE PAPER.

1 2 3 4 5 6 7 8 9 10

To my Father, Americo Michael, who
is forever in my heart.

Americo Michael Giannino

June 2nd, 1925 – March 15, 1995

With Gratitude

I thank God and his angels for allowing me to bring this guidance to all who choose to come and to share their love and trust. As loved ones who have passed are ushered into the "angel room," I know that my dear father Americo Michael is there to safely take them back once they have delivered their messages. Always with love and devotion, the angels bring their guidance in a positive and supportive way. So let us open our hearts now, and allow our special angelic friends in, as they bring us the joy and transformation we so deserve.

Special thanks to:

Susan Giannino, devoted wife & mother
Cristina Burke, beloved granddaughter
Preston Campbell, for all his love and support
Dr. Shirley Snow, Naturopath and friend
Suzi Donnelly, for believing in me
Heather Sullivan, for editing and supporting my work
Mikki Cully, for her beautiful heart and artwork
Marc Palmer, for his design talents and support
All my wonderful clients and devoted friends
Loved ones on the other side...you know who you are.

PROLOGUE

The night was cold and the darkness was evident. He lay in his hospital bed with an angel by his side. His daughter was headed home after the nurses told her he would make it through the night. He lay silent now and waited. He waited for his special place in heaven which was to come that very night. A flash of light, and a vision of two angels carrying him up, one on either side. He delighted in their presence, and laughed with joy as his legs moved freely and easily.

He was free; no more pain, no more doctors, no more needles, no more suffering. They had come to greet him and bring him to his resting place, but his rest would be short, for Americo Michael had a job to do amongst the spirits that were all around him. His daughter—he must let his daughter know her mission. He must bestow upon her the gifts that God and his angels so wanted her to have. He pondered, and asked for help, and so her first vision was to see him climbing towards the heavens with the angels by his side. The phone would ring, and the hospital would tell her that her dear father had passed.

As she entered his room early that March morning, she knew that her father was at peace. The nurse told her his time of death, and the vision of her father's connection with the angels was approximately ten minutes from that time. She had confirmation, as joy filled her heart. She shared this with her mother and the others in the room. They gathered around Americo Michael, and prayed knowing that he was finally free. "Rejoice" say the angels, and so on his stone at the cemetery these exact words were written. Without doubt or apprehension, the eulogy of angels was written by his dear daughter, and so the journey would begin. Cathi was given a unique and special gift on that evening. Her father and the angels would be by her side, and she would channel their love to help and guide others on their path.

AMERICO MICHAEL

SURROUNDED BY ANGELS

A Journey in Transformation

By

Cathi Giannino Burke

Angelic Channel/Medium

Angelic guidance, stories, healing techniques,
devotional poetry & channeling sessions

Sapphire

Communication

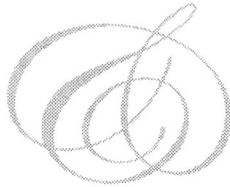

Trust in Giving
and Receiving

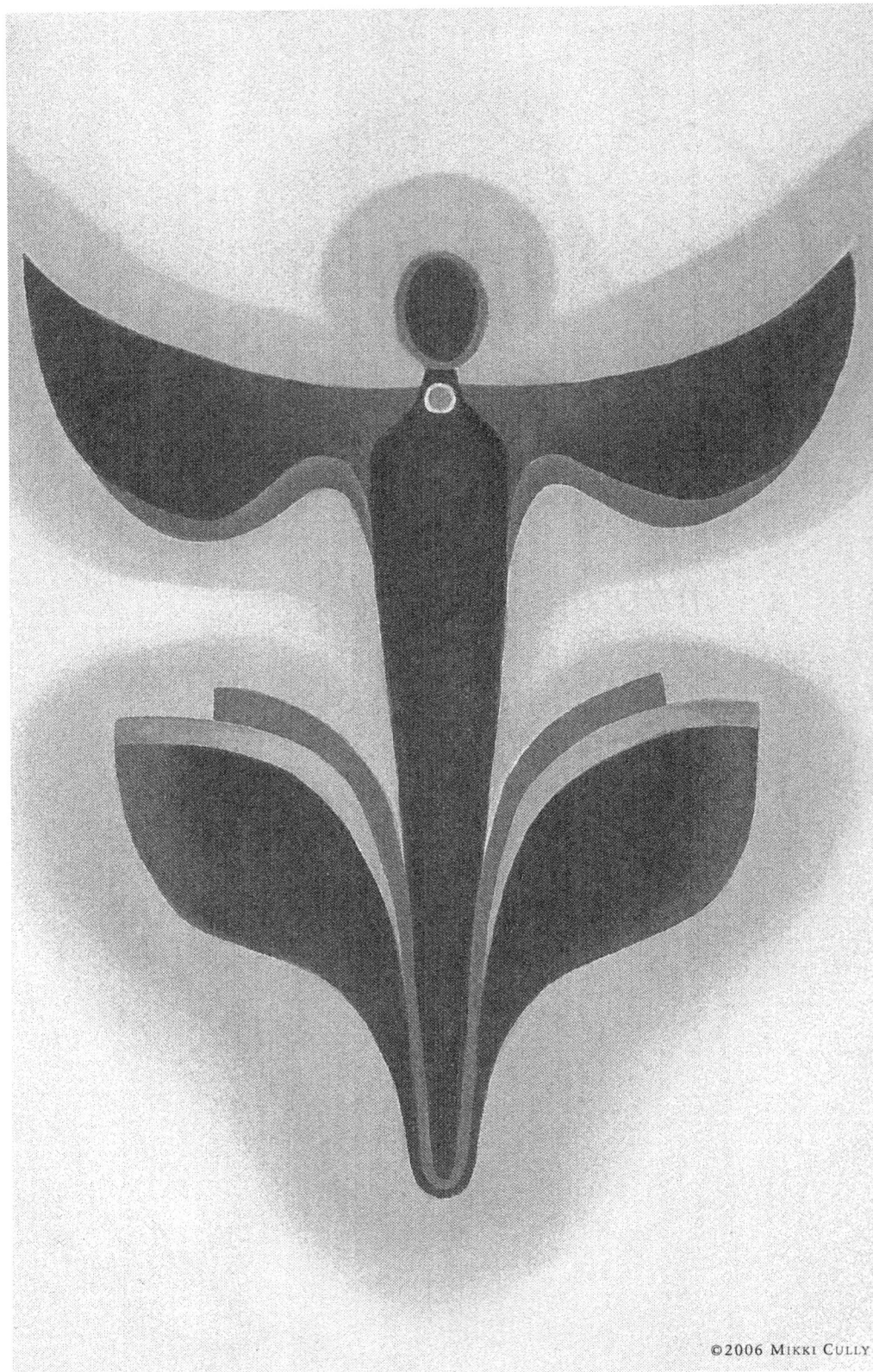

I FEEL THE TRANSFORMATION
THE ANGELS COME TO ME
NO NEED TO HOLD ON TIGHT NOW
THIS MISSION MEANT TO BE

FOR AS A FLOWER BLOSSOMS
THE PETALS THEY UNFOLD
A STORY HAS BEEN WRITTEN
A STORY THAT'S NOW TOLD

SO CRYSTAL CLEAR I SEE IT
IT'S RIGHT BEFORE MY EYES
THE ENERGY MOVES SWIFTLY
AS OLD BELIEFS THEY DIE

FOR IN MY TRANSFORMATION
THE OLD IT FADES AWAY
THE SUN SHINES BRIGHT UPON ME
A NEW AND LIGHT FILLED DAY

I HOLD THIS TRANSFORMATION
AS A GIFT FOR ALL WHO SEEK
TO OPEN UP TO SPIRIT
BOTH THE BOLD AND ALSO MEEK

LIKE THE BUTTERFLY AWAKENED
FROM ITS DEEP AND DARK COCOON
THE TRANSFORMATION FOLLOWS
A FLOWER IN FULL BLOOM

My Purpose

MY TRUE PURPOSE for writing this book is twofold. First and foremost is to channel the love and guidance of the angels so that it may bring forth healing and transformation. I also feel very strongly that every person will derive something "special" from every one of the many writings and channeling sessions. Just by opening this book to a certain page, at any given time the "message" will start to bring "clarity" to all of your daily challenges. Keep in mind that the angels have special messages for each and every one of us daily if we choose to listen.

So let's begin the journey with the angels, Americo Michael, and the many that have made their journey home.

The Angel Nathaniel: Full of Fiery Hope and Movement

How perfect! Since the tone of Americo Michael is one of "transformation." Nathaniel is committed to bringing about change quickly, and in a positive and uplifting way. These are his words:

As I help to transform your body, mind and spirit, I delight in the work that is about to take place. You are open and ready for this, and I have waited; for as humans you have free will, and as angels we must respect this at all times. I invite you now to call upon me for it is time, and the energies are ready, and waiting, for this monumental change to take place. Do not hesitate, but allow these supportive energies to unfold. With splendor, and with zest, you move at a much quicker pace now. No need to turn back for the past is just that. Feel the energies as they usher you to the next level of your spiritual growth. You are filled with capabilities that have lain dormant for many years. The breath will help you along, so use this life giving tool for your progression. Remember I am with you so call upon me often. There is no need for fear or doubt, now is the time to push through the barriers that have held you back. Luck is on your side, and determination is plentiful as you welcome in the life that you have been waiting for. And always remember: One with God, I enjoy a life that is blessed and truly divine.

1

IN THE BEGINNING

Right before I started working with the angels, they were in the background setting up our meeting. For many years, I collected angels from every location in which I traveled. Once my collection began, friends and family members added to it. My home has become an "angelic sanctuary" and to this day I still welcome any and all angelic gifts. I often tell people that one day they will see my home flying above the clouds on huge "angel wings." This brings comfort to all who enter, and my "angel room" though small, is full of angelic energy and warmth. I feel so very fortunate to have been given this wonderful gift, and even more fortunate to share it with those who come and share in the angels' guidance.

As I began to work with the angels, my capabilities grew. Through a series of events, I was lead to work hand in hand with the angelic energies that surround us each and every day. After the passing of my father Americo Michael, I knew I was meant to work with the angels, and several months after his passing I was given a sign that lead me to create Heavenly Messengers.

It was right around early summer in 1995 when a friend of mine invited me to a psychic fair at the Unitarian Church nearby. I was excited about going, and as I entered the church, I could see that the energy was powerful and nurturing. The first thing that I was instructed to do was to put my name in a raffle at the door. Then my friend and I started to go to the different practitioners and merchants who had set up booths on the first floor. Above, on the second floor was where the psychics and mediums were doing their work.

I came upon one table in particular that had an array of metaphysical books and tapes, and then all of a sudden I was standing in front of a beautiful deck of angelic blessings cards. They seemed to be "calling" my name, and as I picked them up I knew they were meant for me. I looked in my wallet at that point, and realized I didn't have enough cash to purchase them so I took out my credit card. I couldn't remember if I had sent out the payment on time, and wasn't sure the transaction would be approved. As the merchant put the card through the machine, I prayed that I had enough money to cover the angelic deck. Sure enough the card went through, and as she handed me the bag a feeling of gratitude came over me.

The rest of the day seemed to fly by, and I truly enjoyed the healers, and the many programs that went along with the fair. At 4:00 when the fair was about to end the raffle was drawn, and low and behold they were raffling off a huge basket full of angelic gifts. There was a lovely angelic tee shirt, angel mug, a book on angels and several other angelic offerings. As I listened for a name to be called I couldn't believe my ears when they said, "Cathi Burke." I had won the basket! Several people who knew me said this is a "sign" and a confirmation. I had bought the angelic deck, and the angels were now confirming that it was time for me to work with them. As I carried the huge basket along with my angelic cards back to the car I felt content, and a sense of joy accompanied me all the way home.

That evening I sat with the cards and felt the warm and loving energy that came from each angel. There was a book with the deck but I only glanced at it briefly, for I knew the angels wanted to come to me in their own words. That evening I put the deck aside, and it would be several months before I felt compelled to pull it out, and look at them again. I was working as a chiropractic assistant at the time, and really didn't care for my job. I had gone to work that morning feeling rather forlorn. The tension had been building for some time, and that very morning I had decided to leave. As I entered my home that evening, I felt as if I had the weight of the world on my shoulders. "Now what?" I had just quit my job, and didn't know what I was going to do. All I knew at that point was I just couldn't do what I was doing for another day. As I sat at the kitchen table, I felt a gentle nudge to go and get the angelic deck. I was instructed to hold the cards and to feel the energy that was emanating from them. The room became very quiet, and there in front of me was my beautiful angelic deck just waiting for me to listen. Suddenly a voice whispered in my ear telling me to hold one of the angelic cards. As I did, I started to feel sensations in my body, as well as to hear lovely music, and gentle loving whispers. I was told not to judge, just listen, and so I did. Within minutes I was receiving the guidance, and love that the angels so wanted me to have. From that day forward I have worked with family and friends channeling the beautiful angelic energy that seemed to flow easily and effortlessly. The angels took over, and showed me just what I needed to know, and for some reason I never questioned their advice. I was instructed to get business cards with the name Heavenly Messengers, and after that it all fell into place. Right around that same time I was connecting with my father daily, and others who had made the journey started coming through. It was funny because if anyone had ever told me I would be channeling spirit from the other side I would have thought they were crazy, but here I was doing just that. It all felt so right and unfolded so easily.

Over the past eleven years my commitment and love for the angels has grown and so has my ability. I feel honored to work with spirit, and delight in bringing this love and guidance to all who come my way. As time passed, I followed the angels' guidance, and different avenues started to unfold. First, I was instructed to do a 12 month forecast with my clients, then long distance readings, angelic parties, and angelic coaching. All of which have helped many on their path. Recently, I have been instructed to do angelic eulogies, and several years ago I was given the idea by my angelic friends to create a special "guardian angel" doll. I had wanted to bring the angels to people in any way I could, and so these dolls were to represent the fact that angels are with us both day and night. I ventured out and found beautiful porcelain angel heads. They had to have a certain facial expression, warm and loving like our heavenly friends. I had an idea to take wired ribbon and make a kind of looped skirt, shawl-like bodes, and angel wings from this wire. I feel as if the angels guided my hands to create what I decided to call "Heavenly Messenger" guardian angel dolls. They stood about 15 inches high, and came in all different colors. Each face was unique, and I made sure to include a variety of hair colors and styles. Each angel was to carry a special message which I would channel from the angels. It was as if the angels knew just what the people who came to my door needed. These are just a few of the channeling sessions that appear on the cards.

I Am The Guardian Angel Of
"Health and Wellbeing."
The Energies I Bring To You Are
Healing And Nurturing.
You Are On Your Way To
"Perfect Health."
Allow The Brilliant White Light
To Surround You, Knowing You
Are On Your Way Towards
The Healing That You So Deserve.
You Are Safe And Loved.

Heaven Has Made Me Your
Very Special "Guardian Angel."
I Come To Bring You A Message
Of Love And Strength, While
Letting You Know That You Are
Being Guided In The Right Direction.
I Promise To Help You On Your Path
As I Watch Over And Protect You
Both Day And Night. Call Upon Me
For I Am At your Beck And Call
And Always By Your Side.

These are just two of the cards that accompany the guardian angel dolls. Again, there are many more. As I hand make each doll, I channel the energies that she will represent. I feel that everyone who receives an angel will become empowered by spirit, and they will feel whatever love and guidance they need in their lives at that time.

These heavenly dolls have been instrumental in bringing joy to people in the hospital or as a gift to a friend in need. They have been there at wakes to remind us that the angels are there to bring our loved ones over to the other side as well as to bring "good wishes" to marriages, anniversaries, birthdays and to guide us through the holiday season.

Once again, I feel blessed to be able to bring the angels in this way to all who open the door to their love. I feel this story is another lesson from the angelic realm, a lesson in trust and faith.

Angels, A Return To "Grace"

Several years ago a friend by the name of Dolly came by and told me about a woman who owned a shop on Cape Cod. The woman had a fondness for angels, and when my friend told her about the angels that I made she showed a great interest. I was given her phone number and we set a date to meet. I pulled together twelve of my most exquisite angels and headed down to her shop. Upon entering I noticed that a rather odd feeling came over me. Being the type of person who gives people the benefit of the doubt, I dismissed this feeling, and decided to allow Yvette to take my angels on consignment. Since it was the holiday season, it seemed the perfect time to have them displayed. I helped her hang them in the shop, and they were visible through her front window. I had also offered to make "custom" angels for anyone who ordered at least two weeks before Christmas.

As I headed home that Saturday afternoon, I had a rather strange feeling in the pit of my stomach. I decided to trust that whatever was about to take place would be handled with care, and that the angels wouldn't let me down. I guess the one thing that did kind of confuse me was that Yvette was very clear that she wanted me to make up a list of all the angels, their descriptions, along with the prices. They were to be sold at forty five dollars each and she would make ten dollars from each sale. She told me that she didn't want anyone accusing her of stealing, and so she wanted everything in black and white up front. I agreed, and when I got home I made up a list and e-mailed it to her. I kept a list for myself, and felt a little more secure about our transaction.

On Monday the phone rang, and Yvette had her first order for a custom angel. She said she had already sold two from the shop, and that at the end of the month she would take all the monies and send me a check. I agreed and began making the angel that she requested. My friend, Dolly would be delivering the angel to the shop since she lived in that area, and was going to be coming up this way. I was also giving her five dollars for each angel sold. This way it was fair for everyone involved.

Several weeks went by and several more custom orders came in, and as each angel left my house, I blessed them with the special energy that they would bring. It seemed that I was making angels daily, since this time of year was when I did craft fairs, and also had them in several shops. I always enjoyed the uniqueness of each one of the angels, and the special feeling that would come to me upon completion. The energies would flow effortlessly into each angel and it was always interesting how the people who gravitated towards them needed just that energy. It was getting closer and closer to Christmas, and as the holidays came and went, I decided to call Yvette to see what she had sold. I also wanted to stop by and pick up any remaining angels.

It had now been several days since I left a message with one of the girls that worked for Yvette, and she never returned my call. This went on for weeks. Finally, after telling my good friend Collette about what had happened, she offered to go down to the shop with me, and pick up the remaining angels. It was a sunny but cold day in mid January, and as we headed out I had that same feeling in the pit of my stomach that I had the first time I entered the shop; dread, pure and simple. We parked the car, and began to walk towards the shop which sat in the center of town.

As Collette and I approached the shop, my eyes grew big, and before I knew it, tears were rolling down my cheeks. The shop was empty, and the angels were gone. We looked at each other in disbelief. How did this happen? Where did Yvette and the angels go? Collette kept her cool, and told me that we should check with some of the other merchants nearby. We decided to go next store to the florist shop since she was one of the women for whom I made a custom angel. When I told her who I was she gasped, and said she didn't know how to get in touch with me but that Yvette had picked up several days before and left. No notice to the renter and without warning. She also told us that Yvette had taken monies from several of the shop owners for custom angels that they never received. She then suggested that Collette and I go to police headquarters and talk to the detective who was there. So we thanked her for the information and headed towards the police station. As we entered the station, we were directed downstairs to Detective O'Malley's office. We sat waiting patiently, and finally he came in with a thick folder. It had Yvette's name on it, and as he opened the file we could see that this wasn't the first time she had done this. She had many aliases, and it was evident that she had been burning her bridges for quite some time. We told him about the angels, and he didn't seem surprised. She had taken monies from customers, used their credit cards without permission, and stolen products, and services from many in the town. It was sad, and I felt that anyone who would use angels to steal must be very desperate. My anger had turned to disbelief, and I was saddened to think that anyone would have to stoop that low.

Detective O'Malley sat with us for quite some time, and then a phone call came in. It was a woman who owned a salon in the adjacent town. She told him that a woman named Yvette had rented space from her earlier that week, and that she was starting to feel odd about it. He asked her if she had brought along any angels and she said "yes". She told him that Yvette had said that she had made them, and that they were for sale.

Bingo! We had a lead. The three of us piled into Officer O'Malley's car and headed towards the shop. As I entered the front door, there before me were my precious angels. Tears filled my eyes, and I knew that through the grace of God the angels had lead us to this place. The shop owner was lovely, a woman with eight children who was struggling to make a living. She told us that Yvette had pulled up in front of her shop, and walked in asking if she had space to rent. She also told us that Yvette had her car full of not only my angels but everything she had in the other shop including another woman's consignment. She was making her living off of other people's talents, and calling them her own. As I gathered the remaining angels, I felt blessed that I was taken to this place, and felt assured, that no matter what the angels were always guiding me. Right before we were ready to leave I asked the shop owner her name and she said "Grace." How perfect. At that point I took one of the angels and handed it to her. She was thrilled and told me that she truly believed in angels and would keep her in the shop. When we looked down to read the channeled angelic message, it was the angel of "prosperity." She smiled and we hugged each other, and then it was time to take my angels home. The detective told us that we would have to come inside when we got back to the station and file a complaint. I knew I had to do this because I do have a belief that what we sow is what we reap. This was definitely a lesson from "earth" school.

I knew that the monies I had lost would not be replaced and that was not a problem. I had five of my angels back, and that's all that mattered to me. Collette, being the character that she is, suggested that I take a picture with detective O'Malley holding several of the angels up. "Kidnapped and recovered" The angels had been returned, and as we stood there for the picture a feeling of comfort and warmth came over me.

Goodness always prevails. Collette had the picture blown up for my 50th birthday party where she proceeded to stand up, and tell the entire story. I have this picture in my angel room, and it is a good reminder for me to listen to my "gut" feeling. Yvette was taken into custody, and was going to trial for the many crimes she had committed. My only hope is that she starts to see that the universe will provide all that we need if we only ask, and that stealing from others is truly a belief in scarcity.

Guardian Angel

I have a guardian angel
Who watches over me
I trust that she is with me
For all the world to see

I feel her love, her eyes so bright
Her kindness is so sweet
Each day that she is with me
A delight & such a treat

She knows I count upon her
The love she shows each day
She never looks away from me
I know she's here to stay

I thank you my sweet angel
For guiding me along
My path is up, my path is down
Your love for me so strong

So as I close my eyes tonight
No harm will come my way
Your eyes, they watch me always
Protection night and day

This poem also applies to all the wonderful male angels who watch over and protect us each and every day.

The Channeling Begins

For many years now I have listened to the angels and taken their advice. I have wanted to write a book for sometime, and prayed that the angels would bring me the guidance to write such a book. My goal has been to always come from the truth, and from my heart, as I let others know that the angels are there for them always. It's as simple as inviting a friend over for a cup of tea, for the angels will swoop in, and provide us with the information that we need. Remember the angels are free from judgment, and only see the love that is in our hearts. As I channeled the guidance, and devotion from our heavenly friends, I could feel their love and commitment. I could see how their only goal was to enlighten, and to heal, and that they are willing to work with each and every one of us. The poems were written from a deep place in my heart, and as I wrote each one the words just seemed to flow out easily and without effort. I feel honored to bring this book to all of you. I hope that you enjoy and connect with these writings in a way that brings hope, clarity, and transformation into your life.

Many of the stories depict loved ones on the other side. They have played a special role in my channeling sessions. Along with the angels, they continue to bring me their love and guidance in dreams, and in my readings. I thank them, and send them my love and light. My hope is that you become aware of your own loved ones who have passed, and that you start to communicate with them so they too may bring forth messages of love and healing.

The poetry is to honor them, and to let them know that I still feel their presence, and that my love and appreciation for them is strong and enduring.

Many of the healing techniques were channeled from the angels, and I feel honored to use them with my clients, as well as for myself.

So let me take you on a journey with our heavenly friends while I channel this wonderful energy, with the help of my father, Americo Michael, and the angels. You will encounter everything from poetry to short stories, healing techniques, and many channeling sessions where the angels will bring you their views of the world. And always remember: ***I am on a journey for my highest good!***

An Angel's Quest

Angels come both day & night
They judge not who you are

Their goal is to bestow their love
Towards humanity near & far

They smile as they approach the earth
They know their mission well

To guide the lost, to protect the small
To watch over where we dwell

Their goals are set & so they come
To bring their shining light

To all of those who open their hearts
And put aside the fight

For love & joy is what they bring
As they show us how they care

So let them in as life unfolds
Let go of doubt & fear

For they are our Heavenly Messengers
And always will be near

Turquoise

Tranquility

&

Boundless
Serenity

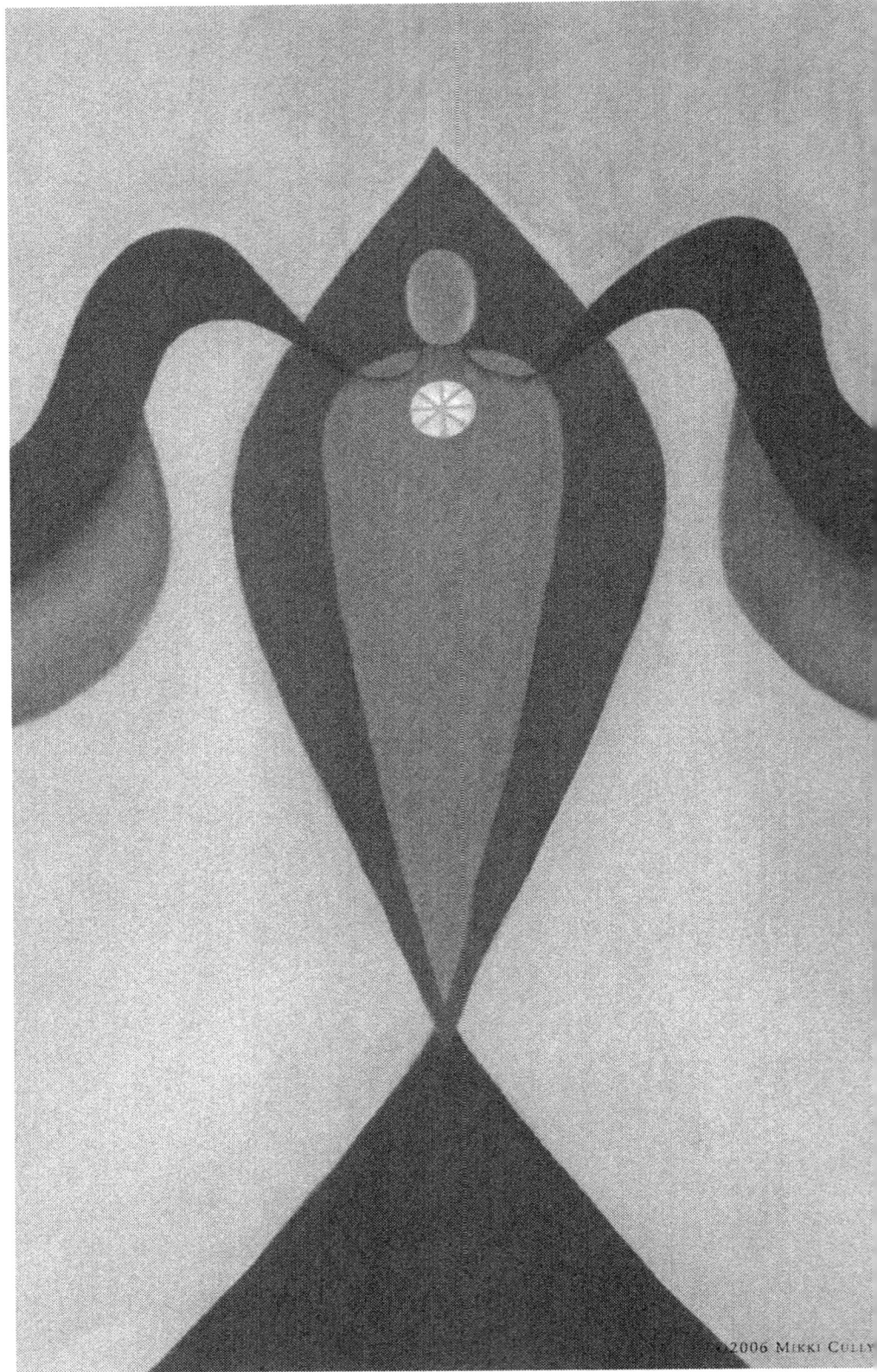

©2006 Mikki Cully

Channeled Guardian Angel Meditation: 2002

This is a meditation that will connect you with your guardian angel. Once connected, many questions can be asked, and many solutions will come your way. This meditation can be done on a daily basis, or anytime you are looking for answers and guidance.

To begin, make sure that you are wearing comfortable clothing. Get into a comfortable position either sitting or laying down. Now proceed to breathe deeply and slowly through your nose. Hold for a second, and exhale slowly through your mouth. Three or four times will help you to relax. Now you are ready to begin. (Putting this meditation on tape using your own voice can be very helpful) Also, listening to this before bedtime can activate your dreams, and bring you many answers from our heavenly friends or loved ones who have passed.

Your eyes are closed and you are feeling very relaxed. Picture yourself in a summer meadow full of wild flowers. Now visualize the many beautiful colors, blues, pinks, yellows, greens and lavender. Now look up at the beautiful blue sky, as you feel the sun shining down upon your head. Take another deep breath and feel a warm breeze pass you by. You feel peaceful and calm. This is a time to release, and let go of all your worries, fears, and sadness. This is your sanctuary, a place where you can come and escape from the pressures of everyday life.

Now look to your right where you will see a small doe waiting to get your attention. She asks that you follow her onto the wooded path knowing that you are about to be greeted by a beautiful angelic being. As your angel appears, you will want to ask the question "What is your name?" Listen and hear the sweet words come from your angel's lips. Repeat the name to yourself, and know that your guardian angel is now with you. What does your guardian angel look like? How do you feel in your angel's presence? Your guardian angel has been with you since the beginning, and will be with you for eternity. Your angel is here to help, and guide you while answering any questions you may have. What is it that you want to ask at this time? Listen for the answers without judgment or fear. If the answer doesn't appear right away, trust that your guardian angel will provide this answer through other people, places, situations, or through your dreams. Be with your angel now, and feel the peace, and serenity that surround you. Remember you are never alone. Your angel is always willing to help and guide you through life's many ups and downs. Never judging—always there with love and kindness. Now it is time to thank your guardian angel for the love and guidance you have received. Wave to your angel, and turn around towards the path that brought you here. Feel the peace, and serenity that is now yours to take with you throughout your day. You now find yourself back in the beautiful meadow as the beauty around you will enhance the peace you will feel for many hours to come. Now take a deep breath once more through your nose, and gently release your breath out through your mouth. Do this several times while you slowly come back into the room. Move gently, and wiggle your fingers and toes, and when you are ready open your eyes, and look around remembering that you now have your guardian angel's name to use at anytime for guidance and support. Call upon your guardian angel often. For it is your angel's pleasure to be of service to you.

Special Guidance

The angels never cease to amaze me. Through the hundreds of readings I have done, I have felt their presence, and their commitment to helping those in need. It's funny but when they want me to channel or do something for them, they are very persistent. Their love is all enduring, and their commitment to helping me is endless. Being human, and having human frailties, the angels have always tried to bring me towards my highest good. They have been there through sadness, and joy, and they have comforted me over and over again. They are our friends, our confidants, our safety net, and above all gifts from God. Our heavenly friends are always ready to bestow their special gifts, just listen for their sweet voices, and feel their love surround you. A special "Golden Angel" is bestowed upon us at birth. Our Golden Angel is there for us throughout our lives offering guidance and support. Our Guardian Angels are many, and loved ones who have passed can also become special guardians to bring us messages of love from beyond as well. The Archangels are a special group, with wonderful healing and rejuvenating powers. One angel in particular is the Archangel Michael. He is there for each and every one of us, as he watches over and protects mankind. He has been given the capability to be with many at one time, and is known as the "Great Protector". He delights in watching over all that is important to us, and is willing to jump in at a heartbeat to protect both ourselves and our loved ones. He only asks that you call upon him, and feel his warmth and protection. I believe the following story will help you to see the angel's at work:

Thank you, Michael and all the angels who protected me, and brought me home safely.

How the Angels Saved My Life

As I looked outside my window, I could see the roads were rather slick. The winter had been a long one, but duty called. As I headed out of my driveway, I could see there were large puddles on the side of the road. I had hit a few on the way to the expressway, and was happy to be getting on Route 3 North without a hitch.

Traffic was moving at a steady pace. I was only going about forty five miles per hour when suddenly my car drifted out of control, hydroplaning and weaving back and forth across three lanes. I was shocked as my hands tried to grasp the wheel, and it was then I knew I was in serious trouble.

It's funny looking back on the event because several minutes before entering the on-ramp I had blessed myself and my family as I do each morning and had asked the angels to watch over us and keep us safe.

As I glanced into the rearview mirror it appeared as if the oncoming traffic was far away. It didn't make any sense; a few minutes before there was a steady stream of cars. Suddenly, I felt a presence, and a voice that told me to let go of the wheel. It was a soft and trusting voice so I did what it said. The car veered toward the middle now, and straightened out. At that very moment, two large trucks flew by me on either side; if I had remained out of control I would have been crushed. I knew at that point that the angels were with me and had saved my life. Michael, Raphael, Lily, and others were there to steer my car to safety, a true miracle yet an everyday occurrence in the angelic realm. Our heavenly friends are all around us, always ready to help. I believe the angels saved me that morning—there is no doubt in my mind.

As time has passed, my connection with the angels have grown deeper and more amazing. I have had times when their voices penetrated my thoughts and the one word that they presented me made all the difference in the world. My father has always played a role in this as well, and on one occasion that I would like to share he was there to help a family member over to the other side.

Sunday, March 10th, 2003

It is Sunday morning, and I was just starting to wake up from a delightful sleep, when suddenly I feel a warm touch, and a presence that filled my bedroom; it was Americo Michael, and he is quiet yet certainly present. He moves with me as I get up and dress and head out the door to my class. I am taking a psychic self-awareness course nearby, and I feel his presence in the car. He sits by me silently, but with great intent, and I trust that he is there for a reason. The class is full of men and woman who want to get in touch with their intuitive nature. Ronnie, the instructor, tells us it is time to pick a partner, and as I look up my eyes meet up with a lovely dark haired woman by the name of Allison. As she looks at me, a smile appears on her face. She asks if my father has passed, and I tell her he has. She tells me he is sitting right next to me, and the message he has will be revealed in the next week. I tell her that he came with me this morning, and she smiles once more as we listen to the instructor.

The day passes quickly, and we are all very excited about what we have confirmed. An incredible exchange of energies is felt, and we know that the beautiful voices that are coming through are "true" guidance, and a gift from the creator. Every so often I will take one of these classes to connect with others doing similar work, and to polish up on my own abilities.

As I head home, I feel as if dad has gone back, and that he will bring his message when the time is right. When I arrive home, Preston is waiting for me, and we have a leisurely dinner, and then head to the family room to relax. My cat, Tiggy jumps on my lap as he does most nights, and seems very content as he purrs, and rubs his nose on my hand. I am just starting to get comfortable when Tiggy jumps off of my lap and goes into the living room. Suddenly, we hear a strange cry, and as I jump up from my chair I see my fourteen year old marmalade cat dragging his legs behind him. I am in shock and call Preston who comes quickly. He picks Tiggy up, and we rush him to the animal hospital nearby. He has had a stroke, and they tell me he will never be the same. My heart sinks as I call out to my father. Is this why you were here? Is this the message you have come to bring? My sadness deepens as I feel his presence, and a warm arm around me. I know he is with me, and he comforts me as I lay Tiggy on a soft blanket to sleep.

Several days will pass as I try to nurture my cat back to health. An eye dropper filled with water and some food by his side. He lays there listless as if all the life and spunk he once had are gone. My daughter Cristina comes to visit. Tiggy was her cat, and she is saddened by the turn of events.

The week starts to go by without any change in Tiggy's condition. It is now Thursday night, and Tiggy lies still on his blanket. My heart is very heavy as I lay my head on the pillow that night, and as I sleep, my father is there in my dream. He is holding Tiggy in his arms, and I feel the joy that is emanating from both of them. As I awake, the sun is pouring through the window, and I feel compelled to jump out of bed, and run into the family room where Tiggy is lying. Low and behold, he has passed. His eyes are closed, and he stretched peacefully on his side. I stroke him several times, as tears begin to flow, but I also know he is safe in Americo Michael's arms. I look at the calendar, and much to my surprise, Tiggy has passed on the anniversary of my dear father's passing! Although it was very hard to lose Tiggy after all those years, I must say that with the presence of my father the day before, and the vision he would bring me on the eve of Tiggy's passing, another gift had been bestowed. This was another confirmation that our loved ones are happy and safe, and working with us from the other side. I had more proof that not only was life beyond truly present, but that our loved ones mingle in heaven. Tiggy sits with my father, and is safe. What more comfort could I ask for? It's been over a year since the passing of Tiggy, and the angels feel my desire for another cat.

I continue to miss my beautiful marmalade cat, but know it is time to move on, and share my home with another loving pet. I keep having a vision of a pure gray female cat with large green eyes. I haven't met this cat yet but decide ahead of time to name her Lily. As time goes by, a series of events lead me to a woman who is selling her home, and has a large litter of kittens. My daughter, Cristina and I decide to take a look, and so we make an appointment.

It is May 15th and the day is sunny and warm. As we ring the doorbell, a young woman answers the door and invites us inside. As I enter the house, I am facing a staircase, and as I look up, there at the very top sits a beautiful sleek gray cat with huge green eyes. She stares at me, and runs down the staircase into my arms. She purrs, and rubs her nose near my face. She is full-grown and the owner speaks. "I can't believe how she ran to you; she is usually very shy around strangers." I feel compelled to speak, and as I open my mouth the words just seem to flow, "May I take this cat?" The owner says she is the mother cat, and I can have her because she is allergic to cats, and must find homes for all of them. I ask her what the cat's name is and she says "Lily!" At that point my mouth is wide open, and my daughter lets out a little sigh. "Well mom, you wanted a cat named Lily, and so here she is." Again, I feel my father's presence as he smiles. He has led me to this house, and here is my Lily waiting for me patiently. As I take her home along with one of her dear little black and white kittens, I know that spirit has once again played a role in this event.

Lily is very protective of me and very psychic. She knows when things are about to happen, and warns me in her own way. We named her baby, "Tidbit," and she has become quite a lovable companion as well. I am one who does not believe in coincidence, and I know that even though our loved ones on the other side are not present in body, they are truly present in spirit, and always there to guide and help us on our journey.

Dad's Advice

Staying focused on your life's purpose is of the utmost importance. Why are you here on the earth plane? What is it that will lead you towards your highest and greatest good? I offer this advice to you. I have been on both planes and see the difference. As a spirit I know that I am light, and love is all that truly matters. As a human I was often thrown off track by the everyday issues in life. Focus now on your true purpose. Give your heart to others, as they will return this love to you. If it doesn't come from them bless them, and move on for it will return to you from other sources. Transformation is what heaven is all about, and this same transformation is available to you as a human on the earth plane. This is a choice and a wise choice indeed.

Americo Michael

Your journey wasn't easy
I watched you in such pain
But then I saw your freedom
The night the angels came

They took you high up in the sky
For all the world to see
You came to me to show me
For it was meant to be

The gifts you bestowed upon me
The night you left the earth
Angelic spirits followed
To teach me of my birth

So as I see you sitting
Upon the clouds so sweet
I know that you work with me
A very special treat

My father he's in heaven
He ushers those who leave
He makes the journey with them
Their souls he helps retrieve

I feel him in the morning
And sometimes late at night
He's there when I am lonely
His presence true and bright

I see you in my dreams
Dear father whom I love
I know that you are with me
Your guidance from above

We work together father
For our purpose it is true
The transformation follows
We have much work to do

And as we work together
I count on your advice
For you are truly gifted
So devoted and precise

I dedicate this book to you
Dear father whom I love
Who sits beside his father
In the heavens up above

Lessons From Above: A Special Angelic Message

As I continue to write this morning, I have a sense that the angels are excited, and that they have some very special information to share with me today. Each morning for the past ten years or so, I pick one angel card from a small deck that has one specific word for the day. This morning it was the card that reads "Beauty." The guidance from this word is of great value, and as I sit here today I know that by day's end I will know the true meaning of the word. What is beauty? In the angels' eyes we are all beautiful for they truly see our full potential, and the shining light of our spirits. The angels see far beyond the exterior, and they know us better than we actually know ourselves. As we go through our day, we can choose to see the beauty around us, in others, and most of all in ourselves. What a relief it would be to look in the mirror and go beyond the little wrinkle, that we complain about or the way our mouths are shaped. What a gift to be able to look beyond, and see the magnificent potential that is standing right in front of us. The angels ask that we embrace ourselves in this day, and that we look at all the wonderful things about ourselves that make us who we are. They ask that we also look at life, and the beauty in nature that surrounds us.

Beauty is everywhere; all you have to do is look at the flowers, the trees, the birds and the sky. The angels have asked me now to surround myself with this beauty that is a gift. It is free, and I can take in as much or as little as I choose. The angels delight, for they know that once they have placed this word in front of me that I will be very conscious of it, and my day will be filled with its essence.

I look beyond the window now where I sit. My cat Lily is sitting on the table on my back porch under the umbrella in the cool shade. The flower boxes are full of impatients in an array of colors, and the yard is green, and lush, truly a picture that any artist would admire. Tidbit is sitting below on the patio, and she is lazily soaking up the warm rays from the sun. Both cats look around the yard trying not to miss a single inch. A bird flies by and catches their attention, but they continue to look out into the yard in all its beauty. All of the many colors, some muted, many vivid, pinks, greens, yellow, red, orange, coral, and purple. I give thanks, and joy, for all of the beauty around me, and will go through my day looking for the beauty in all of life.

The angels invite you to do the same. Whether it is a scenic view, a friend you meet for lunch or that wonderful soul in your mirror, take time today to give thanks, and to see the beauty in everything that comes your way, as you watch your day transform. For beauty is truly in the eyes of the beholder.

A Message On "Beauty" From The Angel Iofiel

For it is with great honor that I come to you this morning. You are truly blessed when beauty is part of your day. Your soul will thrive, and you will know that the earth and the entire universe have much beauty to offer. It is truly what you decide to receive, for the opportunities to experience beauty are many. If you concentrate on the beauty which God has provided this is what your eyes will see. Your body, mind and soul will be fed, and your potential will grow, for you have allowed beauty to enter your day. Now is the time to be aware. Now is the time to look at the goodness that surrounds you. There is no need to look at that which repels, but to concentrate on the beauty in all of God's gifts. From the smallest child to your loving pet to the beautiful flowers to your lover who sits by your side. This beauty is available to all who call forth the energies. Look beyond the dim lights that have held you back, and see the light that shines down from the heavens for is this not "beauty"? Choose beauty today and everyday, and it will be so, for what you choose to bring forth is what will be.

Remliel: Brings Mercy To All

It has been a wonderful week and my cousin Suzi's visit has been energizing and enlightening. She turns back one more time to blow a kiss and a tear falls from her cheek. We are as close as two cousins could ever be. We are like sisters living three thousand miles away from one another connected by love. She waves once more and I drive off, my thoughts going back to the previous Saturday and our trip to the mansions in Rhode Island. The angel of mercy card flashes before me and my mind starts to recall the events of that day. It all started on Friday night as we both lay in bed talking and laughing. Suzi was excited about seeing the mansions. We were to get up early and embark on our road trip. As we finally started to get sleepy and the chatter stopped, a very unsettling feeling came over me. It seemed to be connected to our trip.

I, however, was committed to taking my dear cousin to the mansions so I fell off into a deep sleep dismissing the warning.

Saturday was glorious. One of those bright blue sky, low humidity, 70 degrees kind of day, perfect! We got up and dressed, ate a little breakfast and hopped in the car. We chatted about the trip, our girls, work, and of course, the mansions. I was trying my best to ignore the feeling I had in my "gut" once more. We were approaching the exit for the highway and as I looked off to the right I saw a convenience store with a gas station, so feeling rather odd I pulled inside the parking lot. "Are you alright?" Suzi seemed concerned, and to tell you the truth, so was I. I couldn't explain the feeling only that I felt a bit dizzy and weak and had a deep sense of panic in the center of my stomach. I went into the store to use the restroom and tried to use some of the energy techniques I had learned over the years. Clear my chakras, run my meridians, balance my energy, do some deep breathing, all to no avail. Something or someone didn't want me to go on. I climbed back into the car and told Suzi what had happened. She immediately told me to get out of the driver seat. "I am going to drive home." I apologized and told her we would try again tomorrow. She told me to relax and asked me to show her the way home so we headed back to Hanover. It was strange because the closer we got to the house the better I felt. In fact, by the time I entered the front door I was fine. Feeling kind of guilty I shared what had happened with Preston and my mom who were in the den. All of a sudden Suzi said "let's ask the angels what happened" so I went into the angel room and got the angel deck that I use for my readings and we all sat together as I asked them what had happened. There before me was Remliel the angel of mercy. The card felt hot and was full of information. As I closed my eyes, I saw the vision of what might have happened if we had continued to the mansions. My car was on the side of the road crumpled up like an accordion! I gasped and Suzi took the words right out of my mouth. "A terrible accident!" she said. "Yes," we were saved. The angels had tried to let me know the night before but I wasn't willing to listen. I forget to mention that Suzi is a Scorpio and very "in touch" so it didn't surprise me when she felt what I had seen. A great lesson was learned by all concerned that day. Once again the angels had stopped me keeping both Suzy and I from harm. We rested for a few minutes and talked about how many times that "gut" feeling came up and was dismissed. As fate had it, we ended up going to Plymouth Harbor for the afternoon feeling well and upbeat knowing that the angels once more had watched over and protected us. Thank You, Remliel.

Yes we did end up seeing the mansions on Sunday without a hitch! You must go and see them; they are magnificent but remember to listen to your "gut" before heading out!

Remliel Brings Me A Special Message

As I bring this message to all of you I say that you must listen. It is time for you to connect with your "gut" and know that this tool was given to you for guidance. So many gifts were given at your birth and somehow forgotten. It is time for you to re-connect with these God given treasures and to use them wisely. As if a veil has been lifted you will feel your confidence once more. Trust in what feels right, and do not be fooled by what your head is telling you. Do not please others, if it takes away from what is true. Know that you and you alone have the answers. Trust that these answers will come at times when they are needed the most. First and foremost, it is time for you to believe in the powers that you have, and to use them wisely. I am always willing to guide you, so call upon me often, for it is with practice that you will learn to have faith and trust in the "special" gifts that God has given you.

Along Came The Angel Lily

By now you've read about my cat, Lily, and how she came into my life, but before that there was the angel Lily. She came to me one afternoon when my fear as a parent had surfaced; her voice was sweet and comforting and I knew from the minute I heard her words that I had met a confidant and a close friend in the angelic realm. As most of us as parents know, our children are precious to us. I had been given another gift back in 1979 when my daughter Cristina Michelle was born. She was so small and yet her energy was healing, and her wisdom was strong. She would end up being my only child, and, from the day I set my eyes on her, I was in love. She was wise and beautiful and just about perfect. After the passing of her dear father Walter when she was only three, I had clung to her in ways that sometimes were overwhelming for the both of us. She was my family, my connection to my deceased husband and a gift that was more precious to me than life itself. As she grew, my concerns over her safety grew as well. At one point, I felt a deep need to seek help because I was becoming obsessed with her safety. Whenever we were apart, I would long for her safe return home. Right around the time my father died, I was sitting in the car at Cristina's school waiting for her to come out. We had an appointment and it was easier to pick her up than wait for the bus. As I sat in my car my fears began to build. Did she get to school o.k.? Will she come out on time?

These were daily fears that often lead to a depletion in my energy and had become a constant upset. I had prayed many times for guidance and then on that day waiting for Cristina it appeared. Soft and gentle the words began to flow. "Cristina will be out in ten minutes she is finishing a math test" and so I waited and sure enough as all the other children were coming out of school that afternoon Cristina was not in the crowd. I started to panic and the voice came back loud and clear. "Five more minutes and she will be out" I sat in my car and wondered if my mind was playing tricks on me, and then I heard the voice again loud and clear. **"I am Lily. I am here to watch over your concerns with your daughter. Trust me, for I will bring to you the peace you so deserve."** I had just looked down at the clock to see the time, and as I looked up Cristina came out of the school. "Sorry, mom. I had to finish a math test." She looked at me and asked if I was o.k. I told her a little angel told me she would be late and she laughed. From that day on, Lily came to me whenever I needed reassuring and she was always right. Whether it was time for Cristina to come home and she was late, or I was waiting for a phone call from her, Lily was there to reassure and comfort me. She never let me down. This is a poem I wrote to honor Lily and her love for children everywhere.

<u>Lily</u>

It was a time of great duress when Lily came to me
A time when my entire universe seemed frightening as can be
Her love and her devotion was something I will cherish
Her timing was so perfect, her voice so sweet, so pleasant

Her golden hair was flowing down, her eyes so kind yet strong
Her determination never wavered, and for her voice I longed
She seemed to know just how I felt and comfort was her goal
The fear that often was so deep, the love within her soul!

An odd match to imagine both fear and love a mix
Sent to me from up above, an angel here to fix
She often told me not to fear that all would be just fine
She knew how deep my love had been for that little soul at birth
And how much I would stand to lose if she was gone from earth

For she had been my angel from the minute I could see
Her tiny smile, her tiny hands, her love and warmth for me
I want to thank you Lily for all the times you helped
A school bell rang, my heart would jump, but you were always there
She will be out, five minutes more, a test so don't despair

And sure enough, five minutes passed, and then she would appear
That little girl so cherished, that little girl so dear.
So I must say to all of you, that Lily is a friend

An angel and a confidant, a gift from up above
For Lily knows a mother's heart is one that's full of love.

My daughter Cristina is now twenty six years old, and I thank God and his angels, and of course Lily for all of their love and support throughout her childhood years. To this day I call upon Lily for her comfort and love.

Channeling Ben

My cousin Suzi had returned to visit along with her daughter, Jessica. It was around the 4th of July, and I had decided to do an angel channeling for Jess. We sat in the kitchen with my ceiling fan overhead. I started the prayer that I always do before I channel, and then asked Jessica to pull several angelic cards. After reading several of the angel messages to her, the next card to come forth was full of energy. Over the years I had ushered many spirits over from the other side with the help of Americo Michael and the angels. Now I could feel the enthusiasm and light-hearted energy that wanted to come through. It was a young man, and he had a message for Jessica. As I described him to her, she asked me if it was Ben, her sister Jenny's friend. Just then, the lights overhead began to flicker. She told me he had been killed in a car accident the year before. His presence was strong, and he told Jess that he was sorry he had to leave but that he was happy and very "fine" where he was. He talked about others who had gone before him, and also mentioned that he had a message for Jenny, her sister. The message came through loud and clear, and he wanted Jenny to know the best avenue to take on her path. As I channeled his energy, the lights would give me a confirmation of sorts. It was funny because both the fan and the lights were new, and I hadn't had any flickering before that night. We continued to talk to Ben, and then it was time for him to go back. The angels brought Ben back to where he resides, and the lights haven't flickered since. I think of Ben from time to time, and always receive a reassuring feeling about him. He was a young man who had left the earth in the prime of his life for a bigger and more spiritual purpose.

Ben Shares With All

I must let you all know that where I am is a "New Beginning." It is not the end but a fresh start, and I feel blessed to be able to share this information with you. No more struggle or great effort for the answers are all here. No more searching, no more up and down emotions, just pure energy and love. I have been able to see things clear for the very first time. I look at this as a second chance. I look down and bless those who befriended me, and all of my loved ones who mourn for me. There is nothing to be sad about, because my life is fresh and new, and I am in the midst of spirit that is all loving and accepting.

AN ANGELIC VIEW ON CONNECTING US WITH SPIRIT

Anachel's Wisdom

Over the past several years it has become crystal clear that spirit truly enjoys connecting with their loved ones here on earth. Whether it is a feeling that comes over us, an object of their affection that seems to move around the house or lights that can flicker on and off, it is truly clear that we are not alone. I have asked for guidance on this subject, and the angel Anachel has offered to come through with some words of wisdom.

Chartreuse

Playfulness

&

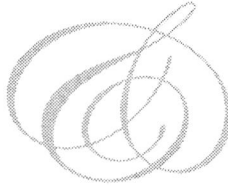

Movement with
Uplightment

©2006 MIKKI CULEY

Channeling Anachel In All Her Grace

It has come to my attention that as humans you often question the beyond. I am here to tell you that what may seem to be light years away is only a whisper, and that your loved ones are not only safe, but truly happy, and filled with joy. As they look down from the heavens they still see and feel your love, and devotion, and they know how you yearn for the day when you will see them again. I am here to tell you that the day will come when you will be reunited. This will be a truly joyous occasion, and one that will connect your souls for eternity. So smile when you think of your loved ones, for each smile is seen, and each prayer is heard, as the love is felt deep within the hearts of all of those who wait for you in the heavens.

Eddy

In June of 2005 my cousin Eddy passed away after a twenty year battle with MS. I had gone to see Eddy on the night he passed, and it was as if his spirit had already left his body. His breathing was shallow and he was very still. His eyes barely opened as his loved ones sat by his side praying for peace.

I hadn't seen Eddy for several years, and the last time I had seen him he was getting around o.k. and pretty upbeat. For the past two years, however, he had declined, and his quality of life had diminished greatly. I found it quite interesting that I had felt compelled to go and see him that afternoon, but I had a great need to bring my mother along and comfort my aunt and my cousins who were already at the hospital. As we sat in his room, I felt a presence close by his side. As I proceeded to ask who was there, I felt my grandparents who had been gone for close to twenty five years. They stood at the head of the bed as they waited to take Eddy with them.

Doing the work that I do, I sometimes find it hard to share with family members what I see, so I sat patiently and waited. As time passed and more relatives entered the room, I could see the energy around my cousin Eddy rising. I felt a great need to tell everyone that they were holding him here on the earth plane, and that they needed to let go. It was interesting because my cousin, Bobby and I decided to sit outside for a few minutes and it was as if he was reading my thoughts. "You know," he said, "Eddie won't leave unless we all give him permission." I agreed and suggested we all go into the family waiting room for awhile. I felt my grandparents stronger than ever at that point, and as we sat in the waiting room, a couple of things occurred. My Aunt Fran, who is Eddy's mother, turned to all of us and said that she had inherited part of the grave site where my grandparents were buried and wondered if they would mind if she buried Eddy with them. At that point, I knew it was time to share what I had seen in Eddy's room. It didn't matter if they thought I was crazy or not, so I told them about my grandparents and that they would be delighted to have Eddy with them; in fact, they were by his side waiting to take him up. At that point, Aunt Fran mentioned that she would like me to do the eulogy. Another shock! I could feel the energies of the angels and spirit as they supported everyone involved. It is so incredible to sit back and watch how spirit works. How angels and the higher self connect through the love that we feel for one another.

Eddy did pass away that night after everyone had left. With the help of the angels, I was able to channel a wonderful eulogy for him, a eulogy that I would like to share. To you, my dear cousin Eddy:

As I See Eddy

As I see Eddy, he is embarking on a new adventure
One that will answer the many questions
That he once had here on earth
A place where pain is un-heard of
And where joy and peace are a daily occurrence
As I see Eddy, he is light and carefree

He sits upon the clouds with delight
And watches over all of those
Who love him so very much

As I see Eddy, his smile is bright
His eyes are full of gratitude
And his journey has just begun
He is excited and full of anticipation

He stops along the way
As he is greeted by those who
Have gone before him
His father, grandparents, aunt and uncles
As he is touched by the love
That is emanating from their hearts

As I see Eddy, he enters the gates of heaven
The angels guide him now
As they show him to that very special place
Where he will live, laugh, and play
His curiosity is great
And he feels the beauty and the light

For as I see Eddy, I see a rebirth and a transformation
And for that we will all be grateful

So do not cry for Eddy but smile, and let him know
You are happy that he has found his special place
With God and the angels for eternity, and know
That one day you will enter these very same gates

As I see Eddy waiting for you all with open arms

Much love,
Cousin Cathi, 2005

A Channeled Message From Eddy

As I arrived the energy pulled me towards the center of a beautiful swirling vortex of light. Colors of all types were forming, and the beauty and splendor are above anything I have ever experienced on earth. I know I am going to really like it here. To all of you who are wondering what to expect all I can say is, "This is truly 'awesome'!"

The Angel Brought Him Through

You could say that over the past eleven years the angels have guided me, and helped me to realize just how close we truly are to the spirit world. As humans, we often think that things of this sort are scary, or that they are just wishful thinking, but through all of my experiences with spirit, I can truly say that they are quite alive, and willing to communicate with us at any time we choose.

In my angelic readings with clients, the angels come through with their love and guidance very willing to bring loved ones together in a safe and loving environment. Healing is part of their plan, and re-connecting with our loved ones is a way for us to complete the healing that we were unable to do here on earth. It always amazes me when I channel a spirit from the other side because it feels as if they are standing right next to me. Their energy is strong and focused, and they have a mission to accomplish, as they allow me to channel their feelings and words. It's as if they have chosen me to be their "spokesperson" for the mission, and I feel blessed and honored, to be able to bring their loved ones together with them once more. One spirit in particular comes to mind. His name is Ritchie, and his wife has become a wonderful friend and client of mine. He has been gone approximately three years, and has been visiting his beloved wife ever since. He has such a strong presence, and his goal is to bring her the love he feels she so deserves. Almost every time she has come for a reading, he is there. Most of the time he walks right in behind her and always gives me a winning smile. "Ritchie is here," I tell her, and she is never really surprised. As I channel his energy, he is like a doting father determined to guide her towards the "right one". At times he will tell a joke or say something offbeat and funny. He has a great sense of humor. I always enjoy his visits, and it is wonderful to see how he is still very present in his wife's life. I have a sense that when she is re-united in love once more he will keep an eye on her, but his job here will be complete, and he will move on in his journey.

Our loved ones are here for us whether in body or in spirit and their devotion is strong. If we take the time to listen and ask, they will come to us with answers to our questions. Being open to this is the best way to have them present themselves. There is nothing to fear for they are only there for our highest good, always ready and willing to help. Their help can come in many forms. People, places, and situations that occur are all ways for loved ones to touch our lives. Being aware and believing in the possibility is all it takes to go from a conscious state here on earth, to other dimensions that exist. So keep an open mind, listen, ask them questions, and you will be pleasantly surprised at the answers you will receive.

Channeling Session: June 17, 2005

Jophiel ushers in the energy of "Creative Power." She is there to help us to bring forth our own "God" given talents as she helps us to develop this creative power for the good of all mankind.

Lessons From Jophiel

It is time to put aside the separation and connect with all of God's creatures, no matter how big or small. The words and feelings that you emanate come back as creative power, and when kindness and love are present then this becomes a source of your creative good. I believe in you, and I know that deep inside there is a special well of power that is just waiting to come to the surface. To nurture this power daily you must call upon it in the following way. The breath is important, and you must use this breath to bring your creative power up. Higher and higher it will come until it reaches the conscious mind. Now sit and listen and the answers will come. Now is the time, do not wait, for the universe is ready for your many talents, and they are needed for the evolution of your planet. The color orange and the 2nd chakra is a powerful source for this energy. Set your goals; know where you want to go in your heart. Allow this burning desire to flow to the surface, picture this brilliant orange energy flowing up, up, up until it reaches the surface, and know that in the right time and for your highest good your desire will come. Always with love, and without manipulation, your creative power will deliver, and you will have come from source.

When the time is right, the angels, along with spirit, bring all that is needed for our highest good. Divine Timing requires patience. Ask for this patience and when the time is right, the answers will present themselves.

Below, you will find a full version of the chakra cleanse. This is a powerful and rejuvenating session that will unblock, and bring clarity back to you physically, mentally, and spiritually. Make sure you give yourself enough time to do this, and then drink plenty of water and lemon throughout the day. This will ensure that any toxins that have been released will be ushered from your system easily and effortlessly.

CHAKRA CLEANSE TO RELEASE BUILT-UP ENERGY AND PENT UP EMOTIONS

There are seven nerve vortexes in the body known as the chakra system. Each chakra is connected to a set of nerves that are connected to the organs and systems of the body.

This is a process to rejuvenate, and cleanse these systems. Each chakra is affiliated with a particular color.

Rainbow

Balancing

&

Healing Energies

The Seven Chakras And The Healing Angels:

The First chakra is located where the tailbone resides
The color is **"red."** The angel is **Ariel.**
This is known as the root chakra and affects our security centers
As well as our self-esteem

The Second chakra is located between the belly button and the pubic
bone the color is **"orange."** The angel is **Michael.**
Representing our creativity, sexuality, and our desires

The Third chakra is above the belly button and resides in the center or
The "solar plexus" area of our body
The color is **"yellow."** The angels are **Daniel and Sarah.**
And represents our personal power and digestion

The Fourth chakra or "heart chakra" resides in the center of the chest
The color is **"emerald green."** The angel is **Cassiel.**
This chakra is associated with "love" compassion
And universal acceptance
It is the mediator between spirit and ego

The Fifth chakra or "throat chakra" is located in the center of the throat
The color is **"light blue."** The angels are **Celestina and Faith.**
Communication and telling the truth is this chakra's vibration

The Sixth chakra or "third eye" resides in the middle of the forehead.
The color is **"indigo."** The angel is **Gabriel.**
This chakra represents psychic abilities, the meaning of life and intuition

The Seventh chakra or "crown chakra" resides at the crown of the head
The color is **"violet."** The angel is **Raphael.**
Representing the connection with the divine and higher self

NOW THAT YOU KNOW THE COLORS OF THE CHAKRAS YOU MAY BEGIN!

First, make sure you are comfortable. The best place would be a room that is noise free, and away from the telephone. Now, sit in a comfortable position, either in a chair, sofa or bed. Next, close your eyes, and focus on the root chakra at the bottom of your spine. Picture a red swirling ball of light residing there moving clockwise. Does it look bright and shiny or clouded and dull? Now, you will picture yourself filling this area with a brilliant white light. Allow this light to flush and cleanse your chakra. Do this until you feel its true color coming back, and then move on to the next chakra. You are cleansing, and clearing the energy from this vortex. At this point don't be surprised if you start to see pictures or feelings flash before you. This is all part of the cleansing process. Let go, and do not judge. Just allow the energies to flow. Now you may continue with the same process with all of your chakras as listed below.

2nd Chakra Orange repeats the swirling sequence along with the brilliant white light **MOVING CLOCKWISE:**

3ʀᴅ CHAKRA - YELLOW

4ᴛʜ CHAKRA - EMERALD GREEN

5ᴛʜ CHAKRA - SKY BLUE

6ᴛʜ CHAKRA - INDIGO BLUE

7ᴛʜ CHAKRA - VIOLET

Once you have finished this process, take several deep cleansing breaths as you blow out any remaining energies that may need to be released. Gently open your eyes and remember to drink plenty of fluids, today to keep your body cleansed and clear. I like to add lemon or lime to my water after this process. This will accelerate the cleansing process, and uncover the stagnant layers of energy.

This can be done daily or several times per week, morning or night. Do this anytime you feel tired or have had a challenging day.

Angelic Homework

As time passed and my work with the angels grew, I was guided to give my clients homework. It seemed so right, and so I listened, and through my readings I have developed an angel homework worksheet. I never really know what the angels are going to suggest, but would like to share with you one particular homework lesson everyone could benefit from. I channeled this information at a time in my life when I was working on forgiveness issues.

A client had come to me in great pain. She wanted to move forward and away from an unhealthy relationship and yearned to be free. I suggested that she start by using the following channeled information. After a period of time she called me and told me she had moved on. She also said that she felt as if her life had just begun. For whatever reason you choose to use this writing, please remember that this is a process, and with some time and effort you can also move forward in your life. I suggest using this once in the morning, and once in the evening. Put aside all judgment as you say the words, and remember to hold your intention. I like to start this off with the affirmation **"I am willing."**

Forgiveness And Release

I LOVINGLY FORGIVE AND RELEASE ALL OF THE PAST. I FORGIVE
_____FOR ANYTHING I FEEL (HE OR SHE)
HAS DONE TO ME. I RELEASE_____(persons name) AND I

RELEASE MYSELF. WE ARE BOTH FREE TO LOVE AND ENJOY OUR LIVES. THE PAST IS OVER, AND I AM WILLING TO FORGIVE AND MOVE FORWARD. MY HEART IS NOW FREE FROM ANY RESENTMENTS, ANGERS, SADNESS, GUILT, SHAME OR FEARS THAT HAVE BEEN HOLDING ME BACK. MY ENTIRE BODY REFLECTS THIS FREEDOM, AND I AM ABLE TO MOVE FORWARD IN MY LIFE WITH JOY AND WITH EASE. I NOW TAKE FULL RESPONSIBILITY FOR MY LIFE. I CHOOSE TO FILL MY WORLD WITH PEACE, LOVE, JOY, HAPPINESS PROSPERITY, AND VIBRANT GOOD HEALTH. I LOVE AND APPROVE OF ME. MY LIFE GETS BETTER EVERYDAY AND ALL IS WELL.

Practice this 2x's daily a.m. & p.m. for best results.

A similar version came about as my own life started to unfold. It was at a time when I myself needed to move forward, and wasn't sure how to proceed. Stamera, the angel of forgiveness, reminded me of the previous channeling, and told me to use the words to forgive myself. As I used this powerful tool, I found that it can make you move forward very quickly. For this reason I use it now every other day. I suggest that you do this at your own pace remembering that transformation is the outcome. If some of the sentences bring up certain emotions or sensations, take a deep breath or two, and just feel them and let go. This is pent-up energy that needs to be released before further progress can be made. Remember to call upon the Angel Stamera often for she will help you to forgive and move forward on your path.

Stamera comes to remind me that often times we do not feel "deserving" or "worthy" so before starting the forgiveness and release process repeat several times out loud **"I believe I can have what I want."** This truly gets the "ball" rolling.

Forgiveness And Release For Self

I LOVINGLY FORGIVE AND RELEASE ALL OF THE PAST. I FORGIVE MYSELF FOR ANY PAIN THAT I MAY HAVE CAUSED MYSELF OR ANYONE ELSE IN THIS LIFETIME. I CHOOSE TO BE FREE, AND I RELEASE ALL NEGATIVE ENERGIES THAT HAVE BEEN HOLDING ME BACK. I AM NOW FREE TO BE HAPPY, HEALTHY, & PROSPEROUS AS WELL AS TO LOVE AND ENJOY MY LIFE. THE PAST IS OVER NOW, AND I AM WILLING TO FORGIVE MYSELF AND OTHERS AND MOVE FORWARD ON MY PATH. MY BODY, MIND, AND SOUL ARE CLEANSED AND FREE FROM ANY RESENTMENTS, ANGERS, GUILT, SHAME OR FEARS THAT MAY BE HOLDING ME BACK. I CHOOSE TO TAKE FULL RESPONSIBILITY FOR MY LIFE. I CHOOSE TO FILL MY WORLD WITH PEACE, JOY, HAPPINESS, VIBRANT GOOD HEALTH, PROSPERITY AND LOVE. I LOVE AND APPROVE OF ME. MY LIFE GETS BETTER EVERYDAY & ALL IS WELL. 1 X daily or 3-4 times per week.

By being willing to learn the lesson from those whom you choose to forgive you are giving yourself one of the greatest gifts on earth.

Stamera's View On Forgiveness

What is the use of holding on to the old resentments that burrow deep down inside of your soul? All that you accomplish is pain and suffering. Release, release, let go now and watch the world transform right before your eyes. There is no need to keep the feud going. This will only bring you more pain. Let go of the need to be right. Let go of the comfort that somehow finds a way into your life. For this comfort is not real and again will only add to your pain. It is time for you to move on to the next level of your spiritual growth. The freedom you will feel is beyond all other and your energy will soar. God is with you, and will show you the way. Ask for the tools of forgiveness, and they will come. As you forgive others and open your heart so will their hearts open to you.

Thank you, Stamera for your love and commitment to mankind.

The Light That The Angels Bring Us From God

As a child I had a lot of mixed emotions, and it wasn't until later in my life that I was to find out that all of these feelings weren't always mine. Kind of like a "sponge" I would soak up everything that was around me. On one hand this is good because it heightens my ability to channel, but on the other hand, it can cause some major confusion. "Where do my feelings begin and others end?" I have found that when I become overwhelmed it is time to breathe, and separate what is mine from what is not. Throughout my life I have found that certain words soothe, and help me to release the feelings that are causing "outside" interference. As time went by, I found this wonderful prayer which seemed to center me and bring me back to a place of clarity and peace. Whether it was fear, sadness, anger, or upset, this prayer, though small, seemed to wash away the anguish, and bring me back to a place of peace. I would like to share this prayer with you today. It reads as follows:

The light of God surrounds me
The love of God unfolds me
The power of God flows through me
Wherever I am God is and all is well

Simple but powerful, these words can ground us, and remind us that God's light is available at all times. I have also used this prayer to surround loved ones. In my morning ritual, I always include this prayer. Blessing our loved ones, and sending them on their way is comforting knowing that God's light travels with them throughout their day. To take it one step further I bathe them in protective purple light starting at the top of their heads down to the bottom of their feet. I often put Archangel Michael and Raphael by their side, and call forth the angels that will guide, and watch over them throughout their day.

Clearing The Channel

The angels also presented me with several other ways of clearing my energy so I could be focused and stay grounded. The way this came about was quite interesting. I was working for a lovely woman in a store called Remedies.   I truly enjoyed working for Suzanne, and her commitment to bringing people the highest quality holistic care was admirable. I would work by myself on Sundays which I have always regarded as my "favorite day of the week." In this little "vortex," I was to come across many spiritual people. On one occasion, a young man came in and we started to chat. Through our conversation, he reminded me of the energies that were around us each and everyday. I found what he said quite interesting since I often had a hard time deliberating what feelings were mine or someone else's. He had studied this very theory with zest, and told me that he himself had similar experiences. We chatted for some time. I told him that I had been given the gift of channeling angelic energy, and he asked me if I had a way of clearing and closing this channel at day's end. We talked for a few more minutes and he asked me to think about what he had said, and then he left leaving me with a lot to think about. All of a sudden the store became very quiet, and at that point I felt a message coming through. It was coming from the angels, and so I felt compelled to pick up a pen and write. This is what was to follow:

Your love for mankind is deep, and can become all encompassing. We acknowledge you for the love that you share. Our concern over your wellbeing is only to protect you, and keep your channel clear for us to communicate.

Then the pen took off.

As a being of light, your channel glows. The energies are full, and so we come bringing you the "clearing" and so it goes:

As you stand with your eyes closed, you will picture an object such as a pair scissors in your right hand. Your attention goes to your waist and you will start at your navel as you cut a circle all the way around until you are at the beginning. You will now picture golden light emanating towards the energy you have released, and then coming back to fill you. Now you will take several slow deep breaths in and out. You are holding a golden key in your hand which you will place at your navel. Just as you would lock a door you will turn this key as you close the energy off until the next channeling session.

That evening more was to come through, and as I lay in bed I was instructed by an angelic guide to clear some of the "old matter" that had been collecting for years. I often look back and see how they were "setting me up" so that their guidance and love could come through loud and clear. The pictures and words are as follows:

Lie still and breathe, for the breath is cleansing and supportive.
You will once again go to your navel which is your energy center.
Your hands will rest on either side, forming a grip.
Now you will imagine a thick black cord coming from your navel.
You will now start to pull this cord one hand over the other.
This cord will display many different colors, do not question this,
for this is all part of the healing.

And so the colors came. As I pulled on the cord the first color to come forth was black. Deep in color and rich in texture, it began to flow from my navel. This seemed to go on for quite some time. Lighter and lighter now until a pale yellow cord began to appear. I could feel fear pouring out of me; it was as if I were being lifted right out of the bed. As it became lighter, another color appeared—it was red, hot, fiery, and it flowed for quite sometime, and as it did, so did the pictures, old childhood trauma, things that were said that were painful and so it flowed. Soon I fell into a deep sleep, and when I woke up I felt light and clear. Upon awakening, I was guided once more to fill the spot at my navel with golden white light, and to express this golden light throughout my day to all with whom I came in contact. I felt like a "golden beacon" that could overcome anything, as I felt compelled to share this with everyone. As my day ended, I realized that it was true "what we give out comes back." The people I had come across in that day were unaware of what I was doing. All they knew is that they liked the feeling that I was projecting, and so they treated me with the love and kindness I was sending to them. Just think of how we could transform our universe if we were to use this powerful and loving energy everyday.

I learned a wonderful lesson that evening, and I now know that at any moment of my day I can choose to come from this powerful and loving energy. A light from above that is available to everyone. The angels now invite you to try this, for you and you alone have the power to "transform" your universe at this very moment.

An Attitude of Gratitude: Channeling Ooniemme: The Cup Half Full

As I ask the angels for their love and guidance this morning, I am reminded of how gratitude plays such an important role in our daily lives. It can make us feel uplifted and positive, and sets the tone for our day.

Oonimme reminds me of this, as her heart is full of appreciation, for she loves working with all of us, and delights in showing us just how much we truly have. Her love and commitment will transform us and will give us the opportunity to open the door for more blessings to come. The cup is always half full with her love and devotion, so listen as her words flow softly from above.

Wake up, and feel the goodness in this new day. It is time to claim your day, and put gratitude into motion. It is time to start thinking of just how lucky you truly are. As you stand and look around, gratitude has begun. So many gifts, and yet so often they are overlooked. Your vision and movement alone are to be cherished. Claim happiness for it is your birthright, and then tell yourself that you choose to make this day happy, healthy and prosperous. Smile often for this too is showing gratitude, and so it will grow. Your day will remain bright, and miracles will be plentiful. Your hopes, wishes, and dreams are closer than ever before when you welcome gratitude into your daily life.

CHARMIENE USHERS IN HARMONY

As we awaken each morning, we have a choice. In that very minute as our eyes begin to open, and we become aware of our surroundings, we can invite the energy of harmony to play a big role in our lives. Charmiene reminds us that all it takes is a quick thought and it will be planted like a seed that is ready to sprout. "I choose harmony in this new day," simple yet forgotten by many. By making this choice we choose to bring forth the people, places and situations that support our decision. What could be easier? The angel Charmiene represents the harmony that is available to each and every one of us with just a little conscious effort. This is the message Charmiene has to share today.

A Channeling Session With The Angel Charmiene

I am here in every minute of your day. Just call upon me and harmony will prevail. I invite you to bring this wonderful feeling of peace into your life. It is a gift that has been given to all of mankind yet is so often forgotten. Do not miss this offering, for harmony will fill your soul, and allow you to be all that you were meant to be. What could be the harm in allowing harmony a place in your day? I will be by your side helping you to remember your purpose, so not to worry. When your day is bathed in harmony, everything else falls into place. So breathe and smile, allowing the universe to take over. You are always provided for, no matter what. Harmony will just make it all seem so much easier. Using the words is all it takes. "I choose to bring harmony into this new day." This, of course, is always your choice but a good choice indeed.

Gold

Truth

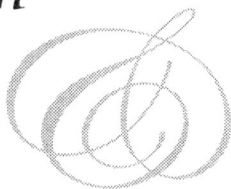

& Believing

Charmiene Presents Herself Once Again In A Poem

The Gift Of Harmony

Harmony, Harmony it's all there for you
Today and tomorrow, there is plenty to do
So look at the gifts that have now come your way
Feeling the promise in this God-given day

To go forth and explore the life given to you
For you are a "present" that many will see
Harmony, harmony, I send down to thee

I guide and support you towards all of your goals
To nourish, and soothe you, and comfort your souls
Your presence is all that the universe needs
For you add to mankind as you plant all of your seeds
Harmony, harmony here for the taking
Harmony, harmony joy in the making
So connect with that place where harmony lives

And I promise you this, for all glory to see
How the harmony flows, for this is the key
For the joy that it brings from heaven above
Harmony's blessings, with God's special love

The Mansion In Heaven

Dreams are a part of our everyday life. As we drift off to sleep our minds begin to rest, and dream travel becomes possible. Many times we have dreams that seem to be jumbled or in bits and pieces, and often times we can't quite remember what we were dreaming about. There are times, however, when we have a dream that we will never forget. I have had the pleasure of channeling loved ones on the other side many times in my dream state. On this cold and starry winter night, I had a dream which would become a sign from my grandparents on the other side. I feel honored to share it with you. The dream begins:

As we climbed the stairs, my Uncle Sal told me to be very quiet. He didn't want anyone else to know what he was about to show me. As we got to the top, he took me into one of my grandparent's bedrooms. The light from the moon was shining in the window and lit up the entire room. He motioned to follow behind him as he opened the door to the closet. I could see a door with a latch and then he opened it and crawled inside. He then helped me over, and, as I stood in amazement, my eyes were filled with color. It was as if we had entered a castle, a mansion of sorts, and as I looked all around, I saw a familiar face coming towards me. It was my dear grandmother, Anina. She was smiling, and without a word, motioned for me to come towards her. As I looked around once more, my eyes focused on all of the gold. A palace in all its splendor. As I followed my grandmother into the next room along with Uncle Sal, I could see that this was not an earthly mansion. It was full of spirit and beauty. Much more than my creative mind could ever fathom. As I looked up in the distance, I could see a small-built man in a suit and hat. It was then that I knew my grandparents were here, together. He seemed to be at the end of the long corridor, and he smiled. Again there were no words, just a feeling of total bliss. I could feel their joy, and an overwhelming feeling of contentment. Suddenly, I turned and hanging on the door in front of me was a dress. It was all lace, and the most gorgeous royal blue I had ever seen. Like royalty it hung, and the feeling I got at that moment was of true perfection. That this place that I had entered had everything that one could ever want or need. Peace, love and joy surrounded me now, and I knew at that very moment that this was my grandparents' resting place. Their special home in heaven. They wanted me to see just what their lives were like on the other side. As I looked around once more, I had a sense that they were inviting one of us to stay. I turned and looked at my Uncle Sal, and without a single word he smiled, and at that moment I knew he had chosen to stay. I told them I had to go back, that my work on the earth plane wasn't complete. In total agreement, they all nodded. There were no words, just a feeling of acceptance and love.

Turning once more I watched as they walked off together. What a perfect way to remember them, I thought, and at that very moment I felt a deep sense of appreciation for what they had shown me. We continued to wave and then they seemed to vanish. At that point, I headed back towards the door and proceeded to crawl through. As the door opened, the sun shone down upon me, and a gentle warmth seemed to surround my entire body.

I had received another gift from spirit. A gift that would remind me of the beautiful "Mansion" in the sky, which is waiting for each and every one of us.

This poem is dedicated to the memory of my Uncle Sal who passed away several months after my dream. We all love and miss you.

Dream Travel

My head on the pillow, a time to dream
Mind, body and spirit become one team
The goals are set in each new day
The challenges come in both work and in play

Yet now I lay in this bed to rest
As the dreams begin, I am put to the test
For dreams are messages from up above
A connection with spirit and all of its love

A special gift from God's precious store
A healing of sorts that we should not ignore
For in our dreams the answers they come
Flowing into our beds from the wings of a dove

Then spirit steps in and shows us the way
For astral- travel is more than just play
So our spirit connects with loved ones each night
As we soar into the heavens, our souls like a kite

A dance so sweet that we resist coming back
But the earth plane is calling, so it's home that we head
We blow spirit a kiss now, our souls have been fed

Knowing deep down inside we can travel again
To see those whom we miss who have gone on their way
We discover that dreaming is more than just play

California Dreaming

My cousin Yvonne who grew up in California shared a story with me recently that I felt compelled to put in the book. Her father had passed away when she was young, and one evening as she fell asleep she awoke remembering a very clear and significant dream. She recalls in the dream hovering above her father's grave. As she looked about, there she saw other relatives who had passed, including her husband's parents. They were all dancing, and appeared to be very happy. As she celebrated with all of her loved ones, she recalls that she had a great desire to remain with them. Her father finally told her that she had to go back, that it wasn't her time, and he insisted that she go back and finish her life on earth. At first she resisted, and then she found herself in her bed crying. She had felt the incredible joy and peace that her relatives who had made the journey felt, and longed to keep the peace and love they shared. Once again this is evidence that confirms that our loved ones are safe and still very much "full" of life.

A Reminder From Spirit

My mother reminds me now of the time when she was in the hospital recovering from stomach surgery. Her father who had passed several years before made a special visit to the hospital, and as she sat up in bed, and looked over in the corner of the room, there he sat. She told me that he was dressed in a suit and had a hat on, and when she asked him what he was doing there he told her that he had taken the day off, and that God had given him permission to come and visit her. They spoke for a few minutes and then he was gone. She also reminds me of the time when her own dear mother was ill, and in the hospital, and how she sat up in bed, and looked out into the hall as she invited all the "people" to come into her room. No one else could see them, but my grandmother knew they were there. That night she passed away. This is all evidence that there is a spirit realm and that they are always ready to communicate with us if we give them the chance.

A Shining Light From Beyond

One of my closest friends, Dee shared a story with me after the passing of her father. Her father, Dick and I had been friends, as well, and when he passed on my birthday several years ago I was saddened by the loss. He was a giving and loving, man who often took us out for dinner, and shared many a good story. One of my fondest memories of him is the 4th of July celebration we shared for almost ten years. He managed a high rise condominium complex facing the esplanade in Boston, and we would all go to the roof top which overlooked the entire affair. The fireworks and the music were truly amazing, boats lining the harbor, the band at the Hatch Shell playing patriotic songs, and the colors bursting into a star filled sky. The 4th has never been quite the same without him. After Dick's passing his daughter was to receive a special message from him. Dee's mom had given her a globe that held a picture of Dee and her father, and as she went home that night after the funeral she sat in a chair in the living room, and as she picked up the globe the lamp that was next to her flickered on and off several times. She wasn't sure what it meant but each time she looked at the globe the lamp flickered. She could feel the presence of her father, and truly believes that he was letting her know that he was fine, and that he was still very much alive in heaven. It's interesting because the lamp hasn't flickered since. This is certainly another example of spirit connecting with their loved ones here on earth, showing us that they are very much alive, and willing to connect with us from beyond.

Here is a poem for you, Dick. I miss our times together, but know that you are spreading your kindness in the heavens.

Fireworks In Heaven

I see you, Dick, so clear so true
The colors now red, white and blue
The boats they line the shore I see
The music now so sweet to me

The memories are forming fast
Of friendship that will always last
The memories so dear, so true
The memories they are of you

The cottage on the beach I see
The lobster that you bought for me

As summer comes it quickly flies
But memories, they never die

Dee, and I, Cristina too
We send our love direct to you
The memories will never fade
For love is how they all were made

The fireworks again I see
The heavens fill for it must be
I see you, Dick, your life is sweet
At heaven's gate one day we'll meet

The Angel Mirh Connects Us To Our Loved Ones In Heaven

The distance between you and your loved ones seems endless, yet you are only a heartbeat away. Your loved ones are with you, and watch over as your life unfolds. They are living their lives as well, and have much work to do. I see how hard it is for you to lose the ones you love, but I must now tell you that they are well and very much alive. The spirit connection that you have made with them is never-ending, and as you speak so they hear your words. They smile as you talk about them to others, as you share the times you spent together. As you sleep, they watch over you, and dreaming of them is surely a treat. You have not imagined a thing for the truth lies in your dreams. As you meet halfway they come, and share the night sky with you. This of course is a blessed event, and when you awaken in your bed you find that your heart has been fulfilled.

Know I am with you, and will help you to make the earth to heaven connection. Trust that the signs that come your way are messages from your loved one on the other side, and know that when the day comes that you make the journey home they will be waiting with their arms spread wide, and their smiles warm and tender.

Gregory's Story

The loss of a child is surely one of the most devastating events a parent can experience. As parents we feel that the appropriate order of things would be that our children live happy and prosperous lives and would eventually outlive us. Two of my closest friends and their daughter survived just such a loss, and as I've watched them start to heal over the past several years, I have to commend them on their courage, and their love for one another. They have shared many encouraging stories with me regarding how Gregory has remained a presence in their lives. The love that family and friends have for Gregory continues to grow strong, and a foundation that provides scholarships for college was created in his name. I myself would feel honored to donate a portion of the proceeds of Americo Michael to this cause knowing that Gregory is smiling down from heaven where he lives and thrives. Here is a poem for you, Greg. May you live in peace and harmony among the angels, as you guide, and send blessings to your family and friends here on earth. If you feel compelled to make a donation to this wonderful charity the address is as follows: The Greg Thompson Memorial Scholarship Fund, P.O. Box 203, Halifax, MA 02338.

Gregory's Home

I see the home where Gregory lives
A beautiful place indeed
He sits upon the clouds at times
Before it's time to lead

The other souls who enter
The pearly gates above
His deep red hair and smiling face
His heart so full of love

With angels he will do his work
"Teamwork" is now his goal
And as he reaches out to them
His arms extended wide
A true sense of accomplishment
He does his work with pride

In heaven days are rich and full
The satisfaction deep
A job well done dear Gregory
God's compliments you'll reap

And now it's time to rest your soul
Upon the clouds above
But first you will check in below
With all the ones you love
(I feel his words come through)
I see you mom, I see you dad
My sister and my friends
I send to you my blessings
Our connection never ends

So know that I am with you
In each and everyday
Just listen for my guidance
The whispers come from love
A deep and lasting union
From the heavens up above

GREGORY A. THOMPSON

MARCH 4, 1983

JANUARY 1, 2001

Aunt M

My godmother Aunt Emma was a highly spirited human being. Her attitude made you feel as if anything was possible, and her energy was positive and sometimes intimidating. She could do anything, be anyone,

and accomplish many different tasks at once. When she walked into a room, people would take notice, and everything about her screamed perfection. She also held everyone dear to her in a very special place in her heart. When she passed away from cancer in 1993, I was saddened by the loss but knew that she would be running circles around most of the other spirits in heaven. She has come to me more than once to bring important messages. I miss Aunt M and would like to dedicate this poem to her. I guess you could say it's my way of saying "thanks" for all that she was here on earth.

Aunt M Comes Through Loud And Clear

I am here to tell each and every one of you that your guardian angel does exist. As I entered the gates of heaven, I was escorted by a most beautiful being, and the love and commitment from this being's heart was something I had never felt before. In my angel's eyes I am perfect, and I felt as if I was being ushered into a sacred and divine place. A place where happiness and joy are part of my daily routine, and where understanding and acceptance happen spontaneously. I feel very blessed to be here.

A Star Among Stars

Her mind was quick, ideas were many
Creative she was a shiny penny
Her large brown eyes so bright & clear
Ideas just flowed, no doubt, no fear

For Emma knew her goals to meet
She worked day and night without defeat
Her home a palace so lovely a site
Ideas, ideas there'll be no sleep tonight

For as she lay her head to rest
While others slept she took the test
Perfection, perfection that was her goal
No time for failure-a determined soul

In her short life she had done it all
But now it was time and heaven did call
We miss you Aunt M and wish you were here
Your loved ones, your home and everything dear

So you now hold a special place in my heart
My godmother, my Aunt, my special friend
So my message is one of love without end
So thank you Aunt M for your guiding light
A star among stars, you will always shine bright

A Message From Archangel Michael

This morning I have asked my mother to choose an angelic card for channeling. My mother, Susan, has a wonderful intuitive ability and although she chooses not to use it as I do, she is still often another way for spirit to present itself. As she holds the deck of angelic cards, she closes her eyes and turns one of the cards over. Lo and behold, it is the Archangel Michael. He stands tall and looks her in the eye, his sword by his side with the determination of a warrior, the "protector" who watches over us both day and night. "Michael," she replies. "There must be a message from your father and brother." She passes the card to me and the channeling begins. At first I feel the presence of my father. He is strong, and his words are loud and clear. He tells my mother that the tests that she is having will not tell the whole story. He says her physical problems are coming from a great need to cleanse and clear old emotions and toxins from her body. He tells her that he is right by her side, and offers to guide her towards the right situations for healing to take place.

He also tells her that he is waiting for her, and holds a wonderful place where the two of them will reside.

Tears come to her eyes, for she misses her dear husband. He comforts her and tells her that he is with her. He mentions the modalities of reiki, massage, and cleansing, and tells her these are the methods of healing that will make the most difference. She listens, and then I ask if he can bring me some guidance on my own physical problems. He tells me to start a journal to release old pent-up anxieties, and to make an appointment with my Naturopathic Doctor. *Your place is here on the earth and you are needed here to help. You have much work to do. You are a teacher and a light worker, but you must step aside once the lesson is presented. Do not over-burden yourself. Know where to draw the line, and do not enable others. This is one of your biggest lessons in life. Teach them what they need to know, then it is their responsibility and choice to put it into action. Like me, you are the messenger.*

I want to stop for a moment now and thank Archangel Michael for all of his love and devotion.

The name Michael has been in our family for years. I feel my brother coming though at this point and he is giving me permission to tell his story.

Michael's Passing

On Christmas morning, 1996, I was to discover that my brother, Michael had cancer. He was living in Alaska at the time with a friend, after his divorce from his wife became final. After reconnecting with my brother after thirty years, it was hard to hear that he might not be with us much longer. He was so far away. I prayed for his healing, and hoped that I would get to see him soon. The following spring I was to get my wish. The phone rang one morning and it was a cousin who was related to Michael on his mother's side. You see, Michael and I had the same father but different mothers. The call was unexpected, and much to my surprise, Michael was in Quincy, a nearby town staying with his cousin, Diane. She told me that Michael wasn't doing very well, and that he wanted to see me. She gave me directions, and so on a rainy Saturday afternoon I was to be reunited with my brother once more. He was thin and drawn, and as we held each other, we cried. He didn't have much time left and wanted to be near his family before making the journey to the other side. Since I was working in Quincy at the time, I would go to work in the morning and visit him when I left work at night. He was slipping away more and more, and as I sat by his side and watched, I had many regrets over the years that we were apart. His mother and sister were often there, and we would talk about Michael and we would laugh and often cry. We had been apart for many years, and then we had been brought back together by an odd series of events. His own father hadn't seen him since Michael was twelve. He had run off and joined a religious cult. There he met and married his wife, Linda. They started a family in Alaska, and it would be years before we would be reconnected. My Uncle Abner just happened to be visiting that year from California, and my father had taken him out to lunch. They went to a well-known restaurant in the Boston area, and it was there that they ran into my brother's aunt. She told them that Michael had lived in Alaska for the past ten years with his wife and two children, Jeremy and Jessica, and then she gave them the contact information. It was a miracle, and one that would reunite a family after thirty years. In 1988, Michael came to visit and stayed with us for two weeks. It was glorious; my big brother was home. My dad had been reunited with his son, and I with my brother. A story about it was published in Woman's World magazine, and featured a picture of Michael and me at the beach with our arms around each other. From then on we had kept in touch for over nine years until the news came. Now, as I looked at my brother ill and forlorn, I prayed that God and the angels would take him soon, and on the night of April 27th, 1997, He did just that. I was standing in the kitchen getting a glass of water. All of a sudden, I felt a presence rush by me like a gust of wind.

The words that came from my lips were "Michael, is that you?" I stopped for a moment and questioned my thought. Soon after that, the phone rang and Diane, Michael's cousin was on the other end. "He's gone," she said. Michael had passed away at 8:30 that evening. I told her what I had experienced, and she agreed that he had come to say goodbye.

On a warm and sunny day in August after Michael's dear body had been cremated, we celebrated his life. Everyone who attended brought a balloon, and we all went into the large field behind Diane's house. The minister said a special prayer, and we all took turns saying goodbye. We let the balloons go all at once, and they flew high in the sky. It was a wonderful send-off, and we all knew that Michael would be in our hearts forever. You are headed towards the light, dear Michael, for you deserve to live in the peace and love that God ensures each of us at birth.

A Reunion With Michael

It's so good to see you, my brother, my friend
I'll remember you always for there is no end
I missed you so much as the years flew by

I wondered how much you thought of us here
I thought of you Michael year after year
Your visit to see us was healing and sweet
Your big-hearted nature, your kindness complete

You came bearing presents so many there were
The picture you bought me that hangs on my wall
The pot full of flowers some big and some small

You told us the stories of your life far away
The joy and the sadness you shared on that day

We spent the two weeks as if never apart
You were always in my mind and deep in my heart

A brother is special and you fit the bill
So, thank you, dear Michael, for the connection we made
A bond that is sacred and one that won't fade

For you are my brother both in heaven and earth
A connection we made, from the time of my birth.
My dear brother, Michael who shines bright as a star
My dear brother, Michael I know who you are

I love you, dear Michael, and will see you one day
When the skies are deep blue and the clouds far away

Lilac

Compassion &

Heart of
Kindness

AS ONE SOWS, SO SHALL ONE REAP

These are very powerful words indeed. The angels come in ways that can help us to see that we are truly "pure" and "powerful" beings of light. We always have a choice in what we can do in any given situation. As I was about to channel for a returning client, she presented me with an issue she had. We began talking about situations that she felt were out of her control. She told me that she wanted to help a good friend in need, but besides putting her arm around her and letting her know she was there, she felt helpless. As time goes by, I receive many questions on this subject alone.

Since we are truly made up of energy, I feel it is safe to say that in this case energy would be the key to helping our loved ones in ways that would heal and strengthen them. Words are not needed in this case, and we don't even need to be present. In fact, we could be thousands of miles away. As we sit and think about friends or family in need, we can picture the most brilliant golden light coming from "source" and penetrating their souls. I have experienced this many times when I would call my Naturopathic Doctor in distress; she always seemed to say the right words, but more importantly she would send a very peaceful and loving energy my way after hanging up the phone. One day, I asked her if she was doing something special after we had hung up, and she told me that she had sent me "divine light." She explained how she sat for several minutes and pictured me, and she also visualized the area in which I was having discomfort. At that point, she pictured this divine healing light surrounding the entire area. She told me that she did this often with patients, and that they always felt better immediately. Since emotions are connected with all disease and discomfort, the light gently and lovingly dispels the negative energy around the area. This brings strength and healing. In reiki, for example, the light is used along with symbols as healing comes whether the person is in the room or not. I also would like to mention that our thoughts do have an effect on us, as well as others, and that what we send out we can plan on receiving back. As my client left that evening, she knew that her best course of action was to send love, and light, to the entire situation knowing that spirit would take care of the rest.

If we send this loving energy to all of those around us, it becomes a "win-win" situation for the world. The next time you become angered at a driver on the road, send out this powerful light. Send it directly to the driver, and then back to yourself. Notice how calm and free you feel. Believe me when I tell you that the driver needed this light, and so did you. For at that point, you are connected as loving and powerful spirits who choose to use this tool for healing ourselves and our planet.

Israfel: The "Music" Of Life

So many times in so many ways we forget to listen to the music in our lives. Israfel comes to remind us that we have to stop, and listen for it is this music that brings clarity and healing into our world.

Channeling Israfel

You are all very special to me. As I watch over and advise others, I see that many are forlorn and over-burdened. I come to offer the soothing energy of music, and the healing that will occur if one takes the time to listen. One doesn't even need a radio, for the music of the earth is all around you. Stop right now and listen, for the birds singing in the trees, and the wind blowing gently through the leaves. Now listen for the soft call of the sparrow, and the strong call of the crow. Close your eyes now as you allow the sounds of nature to permeate your soul. Your breathing will become calm, and your pulse will slow down. You are one with the universe and all of God's creatures, and they are also connected to you. Take time each day to listen to the sounds of nature, and the music of life. A symphony of healing is at your fingertips. Provided by our creator and free of charge. I also invite you to listen to the music you so love as you allow the notes to permeate deep down inside of you. These tones will refresh, and heal your hurried souls. Such a divine part of life, and yet so often overlooked. So as you go through your day invite the music that God provides. Allow your ears to open and hear the soothing sounds. A gift among gifts and free to all who open their hearts.

I am aware that as I ask the questions the answers come. They may not always come at that very moment, but they will appear when the time is right. On one occasion, in particular, Archangel Michael answers my questions loud and clear.

Archangel Michael Comes Through With A Message

You have done the right thing. You have started to trust and have faith. I will not let you down. I am with you, and all of your loved ones. Continue to have faith and courage, and allow me to soothe your tattered nerves, for there is nothing to fear my child. You are watched over and protected both day and night. Many who have passed are with you, and they are helping you with your purpose here on earth. They are delighted that you feel them, and ask that you call upon them often, for part of their work is to support you here on the earth plane. Continue to fill your soul, and listen for their voices for they have much to share. Your gifts will continue to grow, and you will start to feel them more and more. There is only love and good intention in their hearts, so as you listen allow yourself to assimilate their love and devotion. Along with the angels and benevolent beings, they are part of your support system in heaven.

Lessons: A Gift From Loved Ones

Through the angels, and spirit, I have discovered several very special transformations that occur when we pass over. I have channeled loved ones for many over the years, and each one seems to come through with a healing, and a knowing, that they did not come in contact with here on earth. Forgiveness is a big part of this, and over the years I have seen mothers and daughters, brothers and sisters, friends and loved ones forgive one another from afar. It all seems so perfect, for the understanding that comes about is truly a gift and the ego is no longer present. Our loved ones on the other side have obtained a clarity that goes beyond all reason, and they can see exactly how their loved ones here on earth have felt. A child with an alcoholic parent who receives healing through the channeling session and the parent on the other side who gets to complete something and say everything that is in his or her heart. Much healing comes at this point, and helps the soul that is still here on earth understand that it is time to move on and forgive. I have felt it over and over in my channeling sessions, and I feel privileged to be part of this "heaven to earth" connection.

Once our loved ones are on the other side, they no longer look at what is right or wrong, but are committed only to the healing that they can bring. Very much like a cleansing that we may do here on earth; our loved ones who have made the journey are ready to provide us with their love and support, so we may move forward in our lives. We are all teachers for one another, and it is through these lessons that we receive the greatest gifts. It has been said that the harder the lesson the greater the gift, and so the people in our lives who sometimes bring us the biggest challenges are truly the ones that have brought us the most infinite wisdom. Throughout my life, I have had many of these challenges. My own beloved family brought many of these gifts to me. This is not something that was easy. Anger, resentment, upset, and a feeling of wanting to flee were often present. Patience and compassion were lessons that were meant for me to learn. The stories are many, but the bottom line is that the ones who teach us the hardest lessons are the ones whose hearts harbor the most love for us. Like a contract made in heaven before we both descended to the earth. So as you look upon your teachers both in heaven, and here on earth, look for the lesson, and put the ego aside. Being right does not allow us to learn this lesson and will only keep us stuck. You are bigger than that, and if you are reading this book you are open and ready to move forward. I still have to remind myself of these kind of lessons for often my patience wanes, and I yearn to run to a place where I feel only love and peace. If at those times I can remind myself that earth is school, and I am here to learn, then the peace and love remain inside of me no matter where I go. Use the golden white light to bring clarity to your relationships. Surround yourself with this light and your teachers. If you do, the lessons will come quickly, and healing will take place at a record speed. The angel Stamera delights in helping others with their forgiveness so call upon her often. Go back and make a copy of the "forgiveness and release" process and use it daily. This, of course, is a choice, and one that can truly bring you the peace and harmony you so deserve.

The Universe Always Provides

Looking back on some of the events of my life, I have to say that no matter what happened the universe stepped up to the plate. One person makes the journey, and another one steps in and supports those who have been left behind. So was the case with my dear Uncle Nick after the passing of my husband, Walter. Cristina was only three at that time, and now she was fatherless. My heart broke for my little girl who so deserved the love and support of two parents. From the very beginning, another soul would take over and play a huge role in Cristina's life. An Uncle from birth, Uncle Nick will always be remembered for his deep blue eyes and pale blonde hair. Rather quiet with few words spoken, Uncle Nick seemed to know just what Cristina and I needed, and for many years he was there to love, help and support us. Along with my special Aunt Mary who was surely a second mother to me since my childhood, he was there at our beck and call. He has since passed, but our love and thanks for all he did on earth will never be forgotten. This is a poem that is dedicated to him.

Uncle Nick

Oh my dear Uncle whose devotion was strong
Oh my dear Uncle who has been gone far too long
I thank you dear Uncle for your devotion on earth
For me and Cristina, both nieces from birth

So committed to helping when tragedy came
You stepped in and took over and never complained
My gratitude for you is deep as could be
Your support and your kindness, so special to me

You knew just what we needed and accomplished it all
Always ready to be there at our beck and call
In tune with a child whose father was taken
A father on earth who was never forsaken

This connection so deep, this connection so sweet
The candy you slipped her, the kiss on her cheek
So, thank you, dear Uncle for your love and devotion
For coming to us in all the commotion

A ride to the bus and a gentle goodbye
A little red wagon, the hamster's escape
How you never complained
Full of style, full of grace

So, thank you, dear Uncle we will never forget
Your kindhearted nature, not much to regret
We love you, dear Uncle and think of how sweet
One day in the heavens we shall once again meet

Uncle Nick was a man of few words. However, he did tell me this as I asked for his input concerning the beyond.

I feel as if I truly belong in this wondrous land where the beauty is beyond all that I could ever imagine. As I look down upon the earth, I will honestly tell you that as humans you do not take the time you need to rest and contemplate what your life truly means. As a spirit who wishes to help, I suggest that you all go deep inside and know how special you are. For our conversations here in the next dimension are about bringing awareness to the human condition, and helping those who need to slow down, so they may become aware of their purpose. This is one of our many goals as spirit.

Allowing The Angels In

As the angels present themselves in our lives, a transformation begins. If we take the time to listen for their guidance, we are able to make the choices in our lives that are guided by spirit. God has given his angels to us, and their united goal is to bring us towards our highest good. Taking the time to pull back, as we ask for their guidance and help, ensures us a wonderful connection with our heavenly friends. Through this connection, we are able to help many. I'm sure you have all heard of "earth angels" and how family, friends, and even strangers during our lives can take on this role. Each of us has an "angelic" spark within us, and it is by choice that we use this with our fellow man. I always remind my clients that the angels can bring us answers through people, places, and situations. These are the "signs" that are presented to us on a daily basis. When was the last time you were in a store and a book just seemed to be staring you in the face, or better yet falls off the shelf in front of you? I can recall one time when I was going to the hospital for some tests, and there parked right in front of the door was a truck that read "angels8888!" As my jaw dropped, I knew that I was being watched over and protected, and had nothing to fear. For those of you who don't know the significance of this set of numbers, my e-mail address just happens to be "angels8888." The four eights were my father's "special" code when he was here, and when he passed I decided to use it along with the angels. All of these "signs" are brought forth through a network of spirit. We are so very connected, and yet we often go through our days feeling lonely and separate from the rest of the world. If we could just remember to stop and listen, we would hear and feel the guidance that so yearns for our attention. The angelic energy that is present each and everyday is available to all who seek the angel's love and guidance. So make a choice in this new day to allow the angels in. I know you will be pleasantly surprised.

The Angel Ongkanon: Guidance On Communication

It has come to my attention that as humans you fail to communicate. Often for fear of loss, or for looking bad, you hold in what needs to come out, and therefore end up sabotaging your relationships with others. It is time I say that you start to let others know your ideas, and also how you feel. You only need to come from the love in your heart, and without a need to be right. This is the key to good communication. Remember mistakes are few when you are coming from a place of love. Be kind and gentle with your words, but honest in your communications. Let others know their importance as you say what is on your mind. This is because you value them as fellow human beings, and you have respect for who they are. Even those who anger you deserve to know the truth. Without holding back, allow the energies of communication to flow, as you watch the healing start to take place. This is a healing that not only affects your personal life but your planet as well.

Gabriel Brings "New Life"

Gabriel has come to bring us hope of new life both here on earth and in heaven. His words are like a breath of fresh air, and he is committed to helping us realize that the possibilities are many. A part of our lives is about to take a turn, as the doors open for us in ways that we could only imagine. Just as the resurrection promises new life, it also brings us closer to our divine purpose here on earth. Our souls are here to experience and grow, and some of us will take huge steps forward in our own personal evolution. Gabriel supports us and guides us during these times. He knows exactly what is needed for us to make the move, and he ensures us that we will be supported, and that our needs will be met. Our souls journey together, and with the guidance of Gabriel we can make the connection simply and easily. He only asks that we be "willing" to shed the old and welcome the new. As we make this choice, the doors open wide, and the possibilities flow towards us with joy and with ease.

Gabriel's Message

Trust and have faith, for all that is happening is like a stage that is starting to take form. The performance will be a success, and the gifts which are to come are many. You are not alone, and you are certainly capable of attaining all that is good, and that you so desire. Call upon me often for I will help you to see the many avenues that are calling you towards your own personal growth and transformation. The cleansing has begun, and there is no turning back, so move forward with joy in your heart, knowing that the path is right and the outcome divine.

Jophiel/Creative Power For All

As I sit here this morning, I can feel the creative power that resides deep inside of me as it begins to flow to the surface. My 2nd chakra is illuminated at this time, and the color orange is present. The angel, Jophiel appears, and I feel my angel's desire to guide me and help me on my quest for creativity.

The message is powerful and enlightening.

Channeling Jophiel

It is time to come forth and gather your energies. I am here to help you develop that which lies dormant. You have everything you need to create your world. Do not allow doubt and fear to blemish this gift. Connect with this power now! The waiting period is over. Believe in yourself as God believes in you. Whatever it is that you yearn to create is right at your fingertips. You are on the edge of creating your magnificent masterpiece. Your self- expression is growing, and the need to fill this expression with creativity is all- powerful. Connect with your navel. Feel the energy as it flows. It is becoming stronger and stronger now, and the color that encircles this energy is crisp and vibrant. Like a large orange sun in the center of your being, the light fills you now, and encourages you to venture out. You are energized and ready to take on every challenge. You are a creative being, and all things are possible if you believe in yourself. Allow me to guide you. I will not let you down. Allow all of your talents to flow. Your creative power is there for you each and every moment. Put aside the fight, as you bring your power to the surface, where you are able to view and accept this generous gift. Share this gem with many, for by sharing you are teaching others that they too have the power to create all that they so deserve.

Unification On Earth: A Reminder of September 11, 2001

As I sit here this morning it is July 7, 2005. The telephone rings and Aunt Mary tells me of a tragedy that has occurred in London. Terrorists have bombed the subway system, and a bus loaded with commuters. My heart sinks. So much pain and suffering. Since we have very close friends in England, I am concerned for their wellbeing. I turn on the television and the sites so remind me of our own attacks on September 11th, 2001.

I remember seeing the plane as it headed into the second tower. All I remember feeling at the moment was shock and a sense of disbelief. How could this be happening? Why and how did this come to pass? I felt compelled to run into the angel room and sit quietly as I asked the angels to come through.

In silence, I sat asking them for guidance and support on this horrific day. The angel was strong and the voice which came forth was confirming. It was Shekinah, the angel of Unity. I felt a sense of warmth and comfort as Shekinah began our conversation. What will be the outcome? I asked. The voice that came through was strong and reassuring. *A healing will take place throughout the world. This will bring a unification that has been needed for quite some time. Many will feel the energies of brotherhood even if it is for a short period of time for good always prevails over evil. The many souls who have come towards the heavens are being ushered in by the light, and their fears and pain have been dissolved. It is our job now to comfort those on earth who have lost their loved ones, and to bring forth a connection with all of humanity.* This clear and defined message played out over the world as nations from every corner of the globe came together to support each other. For a moment we were all one. The political parties were united and on the same side for the first time in history, and our neighbors and friends became the instruments for the many vigils that took place around the world. Candles were lit and the healing light of God was everywhere. There were stories from the World Trade Center of angels, and how people who were trapped without any hope of survival were somehow guided by a voice or a hand that reached out and showed them the way.

We must believe that although this tragedy was one of great proportion, it was also a time of healing and faith. As Americans, our commitment to freedom has been re-established and our love for our country has been affirmed. As I sit here this morning and see the tragedy in London, it reminds me once again that we must all pull together, and truly look at what is important in life. That just waking up in the morning with all of our senses intact is a gift beyond all gifts. These are but a few of the many miracles happening all around us each and every day. It is truly up to us to open our hearts and minds to these gifts, and to acknowledge and show gratitude on a daily basis.

I send my love and support along with the healing light of the Holy Spirit to our brothers and sisters in England. May they find peace and comfort out of this tragedy, and may they find their way towards the miracles that are present here on earth and in heaven.

The Angels Remind Us All

Working with the angels has brought me closer to my true self. I have learned many wonderful things about myself and others with the gentle and supportive love of our heavenly friends.

One very special gift I have learned is that we truly are pure energy.

As humans, we have chosen our earthly bodies to experience the lessons that our soul must learn. Somehow we seem to forget, however, that we are holding within us an immense amount of electrical energy that can be used to express, to promote and, most of all, to heal. As time goes by, we are starting to work with this incredible resource more and more. The angels remind us that we are very capable of harnessing this energy and that the use of these subtle, yet powerful energies is a choice that we have every day of our lives. Being responsible for these energies is paramount.

For example, one very powerful source of this energy is our thoughts; another would be our tongue—that which flows from our lips, and another would be our body language. As we go through our day, we must remind ourselves of this power and use it wisely. Stop for a moment, and think about just how powerful the spoken word is. The telephone rings, and you answer it. At that very moment, your tone of voice holds the key to the entire conversation. Will you speak gently in a kind manner with supportive words, or will you lash out at your neighbor spreading rumors and gossip? These are the choices we have in our midst each and every moment.

If we use this God-given energy to promote goodness, compassion and love, then that is what we will receive in return. You may ask yourself this question, "Do I deserve to be treated with love and support?" or "Should I expect others to be kind to my face yet be non-supportive and disrespectful behind my back?" This is a very important question to ask. "How am I contributing to these situations?" and "How can I become the light, and love that each and every one of us has inside?" This, to me, is one of the biggest challenges on the earth plane. To watch and guide our thoughts and speech to bring healing, and to promote unity on our planet, or to tear down others thereby causing the separation that we so often feel. Each and every day we have a choice.

As humans, we have certain emotions and beliefs that, at times, get in the way of our "highest" use of these energies, but as we grow and learn we can turn our thoughts over to what is truly divine, becoming a guiding light for all who cross our path.

Like the angels, we bring about soothing and peaceful energy to all who decide to connect with us, and in return, we receive the gift of peace, and a connection with all of mankind.

The Spoken Word

In this new day I have a choice
I know that this is true
My thoughts I tune my speech with love

I send the "best" to you
For as I think about the earth
And yearn for peace to flourish
I remind myself that it starts with me
For I am the one who will nourish

The energies that flow right now

Are full of love and peace
The wars they stop
The fighting ends
And for this I release

The sadness that lies deep inside
For all mankind to see
The energies flow, the energies flow
I have chosen this path to be

For I am here to help earth heal
Sent from up above
To soothe mankind and bring back hope
Remembering God's true love

The light I shed upon the earth
Returns to me ten-fold
And so I make the choice this day
With energy fresh and bold

I send you love, I send you light
My brother, sister, friend
For earth is home and so we live
Our souls are here to mend

So show your love in this new day
Be bold as you can be
For as you give it returns to you
A celebration for all to see

Channeling Hadraniel: Angelic Love

So many times we wonder "Why do people treat me the way they do?" and "Why do the same patterns keep coming up in my life?" These are questions that can often be very tough to answer. As I sit here this morning, the angel, Hadraniel has offered to come through and bring us some insight into these very questions.

Deep inside each and every one of you is a special and guarded place.

Like the core which resides deep inside the earth you have a choice right now to come from source. As you forego the ego, and look deep within yourself, you will find perfection beyond anything you could ever imagine. I, Handraneil, invite you to call upon this core, as you invite this magnificent energy into your daily life. You are so much more than you realize. The difference that you make is paramount, and the time you spend dwelling on the issues in your life will only drain you, and lead you into the illusion that your life is worthless and shallow. On the contrary, you are pure love, and this love can emanate from you at all times. The key is to first love yourself and to embrace all that you are. Connect with the kindness in your heart knowing that your actions lead to the outcome. Know that you are perfection at all times. As you claim this perfection others will become connected as well. The time has come to hold your head up high, and to develop this love in a way that is nurturing and powerful. Slow down, be with yourself, acknowledge your accomplishments, and sit in silence knowing that God and his angels are a big part of this love. In your perfection, bless yourself. Thank yourself for all that you do each and every day. Fall in love with the person on the other side of the mirror. Court yourself, and talk with kind and loving words. Go forth in your day with a sense of renewal, knowing that you and you alone can make a difference. Your reward will be evident as the people around you will shift and feel the love. In turn, it will emanate back to you. Call upon me to guide you, for I am Hadraniel, the angel of love, and your presence on earth is special, for your spirit is ready to flourish in your newfound love, and appreciation for who you truly are. For always remember that you are a child of God, and his love for you is never ending.

I Know Who I Am

The morning comes, my rest is over
My dreams were many a field of clover
I saw myself in a special way
A pure connection to start my day

For in my dream the truth came forth
My soul spoke out and shared with me
The love and perfection that was to be

I embraced myself in a different way
I embrace myself with love, I say
I watched my aura as it began to shed
The old beliefs, the doubt, the dread

I saw that I was so much more
Than all the ideas that I seemed to live for
I can see through the fog for it has been lifted
The pure love and devotion at last it has shifted
So kindness follows for all mankind
So special gifts now come my way
Since I have embraced myself today

I feel the love deep in my core
I feel the love I can no longer ignore
A gift, a gift, from up above
A gift from God, a gift of love

So as I awaken in this new day
I no longer have the price to pay
For thinking that I must be better
I know myself down to the letter

So I invite you now to take my hand
Together we will walk in this new land
Knowing that we both are just pure love
Accepting this truth from heaven above

<u>444</u>

As I continue to do my work with the angels, I have come across some very interesting information. In the beginning, all I was aware of was that I had a deep passion for collecting angels as well as a growing interest in anything that had to do with the angelic realm. As time went by, I learned many new and interesting things about angels and how they work. One very interesting concept that I fell upon through the information that a close friend provided was that the numbers 444 in that order meant that the angels were present. It was very interesting because as I started to watch this particular number, the presence of the angels grew. I would be driving in the car and for no particular reason I would look at the clock and the time would be 4:44. "Ah, the angels are present." One day, I was writing out my social security number and right in the middle were the numbers 444. Coincidence? I have to be honest with you; at first, I thought it might be but as I grow and learn more and more about life I truly feel that there is no such thing as a "coincidence." Was I destined to work with the angels since birth? Was it all predestined, and then when my father passed over to the other side the gift would unfold? Was it truly "divine timing?" Again, I believe that everything that happens in our lives is meant to happen. It is, of course, our choice to accept this gift or turn our backs on it. I have fully embraced my work with the angels, and I am committed to bringing our heavenly friends to as many people as possible. So if my social security number is a "hint," then I will gladly accept the clue, as I continue to work with the angels sharing their love, and guidance with all who open their hearts.

444 Shows Up Again

Several years after my grandparents passed, my mother had a dream that my grandparents were sending her a message. In that message they kept showing her the number 4. My grandmother was ironing 4 pairs of pants, and my grandfather was holding up 4 fingers. When my mother told me, I said that I felt they were trying to send her a message, and that she should watch for the number 4. Well, lo and behold, the number did present itself that very day. She had gone to the local variety store to buy a ticket, hoping she would win some extra money. It was right before Christmas, and she was a little low on cash. I'll never forget how she scratched the ticket and the number 4 came up three times, and each time she had won. Once again, the angels had presented themselves, in this case, through her parents on the other side. She actually won $400.00 on 444! Could it be that our loved ones on the other side are working with our heavenly friends? I believe that there is a force of spirit that works in many ways to support our human effort here on earth. A kind of "light" that emanates down from God, his angels, saints, benevolent beings, spirit guides, and of course, our loved ones who have made the journey home. It's funny but when most people think of angels they only think of them as guardians, and helpers that can save us from harm. I feel that they are so much more, and are willing to help us in all areas of our lives. They come to bring us their love, along with healing, forgiveness, prosperity, love, joy and comfort. The angels are there each and every day for us to call upon for help. Like a good friend, our angels come to us in the "real" world providing love and support when we are in need. How will your angels present themselves in your life today? Remember that they are willing to help so all we really have to do is ask. Whether it's our health, a mortgage that is going to be late or watching over our loved ones, the angels are more than happy to bring us closer to our hopes and dreams. So the next time you see 444 in a row, know that your angels are with you, and that they are trying to tell you that they are willing to help you in any way that they can in that very moment. Remember to call upon them often, for they delight in the sound of your voice.

Emerald

Abundance

&

Knowing All is Infinite Wealth

CHANNELING FORTUNATA: PROSPERITY IS ALWAYS AVAILABLE

I am here for you these are the words that come this morning as I channel the love and prosperity that that angel Fortunata brings. She is so devoted to us in many ways and truly wants us to flourish and be happy. The colors that she exhibits are pink, purple, light blue and pale green. Her hand is lifted as she bestows the many blessings that are coming your way. Are you ready for her kind and generous gifts?

Prosperity awaits you. Open your arms and embrace this gift. You have worked hard, and deserve all that is good. Do not turn your back for it is with love that these gifts are brought to you. Doubts and fears will only hold you back now, so erase them as they present themselves. My gifts are packaged and ready to be sent. Open your arms, receive the goodness that flows your way. Show gratitude, and more will come. I am delighted in watching your smile. Please allow me in, so that I may bring you all that you so deserve.

Fortunata brings us these gifts with pure love and devotion. She knows exactly what we need, and so the gifts are many. A new place to live, a wonderful loving relationship, seeing our children happy and prosperous, a job that we truly love-these are but a few of the things that are considered "prosperity" in the eyes of the angels. Money is a big part of prosperity as well, and if needed will flow down upon you in ways you might never imagine. Honor the gifts that have already come your way. Acknowledge their presence and more will follow. Know that it is perfectly fine to receive, and be willing to do this with open arms. Remember that all that you have put out into the universe in the way of love and kindness returns to you. Be pure of heart, and give this out as Fortunata does. Your kind acts will be rewarded by spirit and Fortunata will bestow upon you all the prosperity that you will ever need or want.

During one of my 12 month forecasting sessions the angel Fortunata instructed me to use this "clearing" with a client who was great at giving but not very open to receiving.

Opening The "Receiving" Channel

Find a cozy spot where you can be away from noise and the telephone. Sit in a comfortable position and take 3-4 cleansing breaths. You will start to feel relaxed. At this point make sure your hands are resting in an upright position on your legs. Next, scan your body for any resistance and if you do feel some then breathe again. Repeat the following sentence several times. "I, _____ (your name) now give the angel Fortunata permission to bring "prosperity" into my life. As you do this you may feel a warmth or tingling sensation in your body. This is the "divine energy" starting to surround your aura. You are now ready to receive. Open your arms now so they stretch out on both sides as you extend them up to the heavens; look up now and claim your gifts. These are the words: I, _____ (your name) am now willing to receive all the love, all the joy, all the happiness, all the peace, all the prosperity, all the good health, all the success, and all of the healing that the universe has to give. You have claimed your gifts. It is time to pull your arms in and hug yourself. You have now embraced what you have claimed. Now see how that feels. Do it several more times and watch how your day unfolds. Remember that these are gifts from God, and it would be a shame not to allow them in. Enjoy!

"The blessings of the Lord makes rich, and he adds no sorrow with it." Proverbs 10:22

The Archangel Michael is around us a lot more than we know. This morning he invites me to share this channeling session with all of you.

A Message From The Archangel Michael

Through my commitment to your loved ones, I spread my protection, for it is what I am to do for all of mankind. Please call upon me often, and I will make sure that both you and your loved ones are safe. I will stand by their side, and hold my sword up for their protection. Turn your worries and fears over to me, for I will shield all who ask for my guidance and protection. This is my commitment to all of humanity.

Hamied Steps In: An Offering From Hamied Who Ushers In Miracles

Today is a new day; this is another gift from the universe. A miracle that is often overlooked. Use this day to allow miracles to unfold. Believe that all is possible, trust and have faith. Know that I am with you helping you to understand that miracles are all around you. Embrace this now, as you watch for the many miracles that, as humans, you often overlook. As you become aware, you will start to see that a true miracle is right in front of you, and you will begin to feel the love and devotion that spirit has to share. Count your blessings daily, and as you do, these miracles will appear.

A Channeled Poem From Hamied

Daily Miracles

Miracles, miracles everywhere
Miracles, miracles so do not despair
Miracles, miracles for all to see
A day full of miracles for it must be
For life is given in this new morn
For life is given from dusk to dawn

The miracles they flow from up above
The miracles they flow from God's pure love
For all of you in this new day
The miracles come without delay
If you just would stop for a minute or two
The miracles would appear without ado
So watch for miracles, they are everywhere
So watch for miracles, and do not despair
Right under your nose the miracles come
The miracles, miracles, one by one
So receive the miracles in this new day
Miracles, miracles so don't despair
Miracles, miracles are everywhere
So open your arms as the miracles flow
From the heavens above, to the earth down below

Ariel Brings Us "Nature" In All Its Splendor

Ariel has come through this morning with a message for all of us. She offers her advice and can only hope that the choices we make are for our highest good. She asks that we take some time to look over our daily routines and that we consider the consequences of our actions. *Your soul resides within your body, and the body must be nourished, and taken care of in order for the soul to do its work.* These are her "special words." She asks that we scan our bodies and see where we are low in energy and vitality. *Listen and you will know what to do. Take time to consider making changes in your daily routine to support your purpose!* She is a true advocate of a natural and healthy diet along with lifestyle changes that promote health and vitality. *It is through your efforts to be "whole" that I support you on your path. It is your choice to support and nourish your bodies with all that is pure and simple. Like a well-oiled machine, the body also needs the "right" components to take you where you want to go.* The body is a reflection of your thoughts, desires, hopes, and dreams. You hold the key to longevity and wellbeing. So Ariel once again asks that you stop and take a look at what you are putting into your body and your mind. Whether it is food or thought, the choice is yours and yours alone. She asks that you make the changes that will lead to perfect health and that you also share these changes with others. *Put back into the universe what you have learned. Give this gift back to your fellow human beings, and watch the goodness return to you, for that which you give out comes back. You are a shining example for your friends and loved ones. The body is an amazing machine that houses the soul. Cherish your body. Feed it nourishing foods and beverages. Take time to stretch and relax. This is your temple on earth. So clean your temple often and feed it as you would a precious child, for that is truly who you are.*

Susan Beth

The news of my sister's passing was both shocking and sad. Her life was taken at an early age, and although I know she is with God and his many angels, my heart still feels the loss. My sister and I had our ups and downs, and there were times when I didn't like what was happening in her life. Through all of this, my love for her remained strong and enduring.

There are many types of love in this world, but the love for a sister is very special and never fades. I know her love for me was there even when times were rough. The first time I saw Susan Beth was in the bassinet in our living room in Weymouth. My eyes widened as I looked down upon the little baby girl with the big brown eyes and dark fuzzy hair. I felt a sense of warmth and love envelop me, and I felt I would never be alone again.

As she grew, she became my protector, and she would turn the lights on for me in a dark room, and step on the bugs that frightened me. I remember her saying, "Don't be afraid, Cathi; I won't let that spider hurt you."

We spent many hours playing together, and as time passed, I watched my sister grow into a very pretty little girl. One time in particular stands out in my mind. It was one summer afternoon in our backyard in Braintree. We would often put on shows in the backyard and on one occasion Suzy stood up and sang the song "I'm just wild about Harry," her little body swaying back and forth and her big brown eyes rolling around. We all clapped and told her she should be on TV. She won the talent contest that day. I also remember that she loved school a lot more than I did and was a straight "A" student. She would study for hours, and never missed a day no matter how sick she felt. I remember how she loved to be outside, and would play in the snow for hours, coming in the house like an icicle only to change her mittens and go outside for more. One memory in particular is how she stuck close by my mother's side, and followed my mother everywhere. My mother nick- named her "armpit Sadie," a name that followed her for years. We were very close growing up and I remember that when I started dating she was devastated thinking she had lost me forever. Through all of this, my love for her remained strong.

I remember the day she graduated from high school and how proud I was of her. We celebrated her special day, and we were hopeful for the future. She was beautiful, and modeling school came next and the pride grew. Her potential was great, and I wished her all the luck in the world. She was the maid of honor at my wedding, and my daughter's godmother. I know this meant the world to her. As life passed by and we grew older, there were many changes in both of our lives. Many lessons were presented to us, and many times they were not easy. Throughout all of this, our love for each other prevailed. I learned many lessons from my sister, and for that I am grateful.

She taught me patience and forgiveness, and in a way she taught me a lot about love and devotion, as well. I had a dream a short time after the passing of Susan Beth. I know she would want me to share this in my book. The dream begins: Suzy and I were children again and it was wintertime. Our laughter was jubilant as we flew down the hill together on our sleds. We fell over and got covered with snow, and we got up and shook ourselves off, and headed up the hill for more. Over and over again, we proceeded up the hill and down again with laughter and delight. I remember feeling so free, a feeling that I would remember for the rest of my life. When I woke up, I knew I had been there with my little sister on that hill once more, laughing and loving the time we spent together. I would call that astral-travel at its best!

In high school many of her friends called her "Suzy Q." Here is a poem I dedicate to you "Suzy" with love and gratitude.

Suzy Q.

It's time my sister to say goodbye
I know you would like to stay
But heaven calls this very night
And so you must obey

The angels come and take you up
So very high indeed
The clouds, they part, the light shines through
Your body, soul, impede

A time of peace and love returns
Your soul finally at rest
But not for long, dear sister
For now you have a quest

To work for God in heaven
That is your job I see
To guide the small and frightened
Your love will set them free

For just like you the time has come
For them to leave the earth
My sister and my confidant
Sisters from our birth
I talk to you often
I know you hear me, sis
With kindness and devotion
Your love I truly miss

The nights you come to visit
You bring your words unspoken
I visit you from time to time
In dreams that show the token

For sister we will always have
A special love you see
My little sister, Suzy Q
In heaven you are free

This is a channeling session I had one afternoon with Suzy. I had asked her what her perception of heaven was and this is what she said.

Suzy At Play

We take time to play here in what you humans call "heaven." It is a daily occurrence, and the balance between work and play is something that you are taught from the moment you enter the gates. Most of you on earth do not take the time to play, and that in God's eyes is a shame. We are expected to take time to laugh and feel joy as we mingle with others who have made the journey. Our work is very pleasurable, and we blend with one another in harmony and love. I feel very honored to be here, as I send blessings down to all of my loved ones.

Thoughts Are Creative

For many years I have worked on myself. My body has always been a great lesson for me from the very beginning, and I have diligently tried for many years to lose weight. Over a period of time after many different diets and exercise plans, I had dropped over sixty pounds, and finally my dream of being "thin" had come true. At the tender age of nineteen, I weighed a svelte 117 pounds. I had finally reached my goal, and for almost twenty years was able to stay within ten or twelve pounds of that weight. At age fifty-one, I am a bit heavier, and probably will never see 117 pounds again, but then the angel Metatron reminds me of the power of thought as he comes to teach us that "thoughts are things" and what we think we will eventually create. I am reminded of the power of thought now, and how it can turn our lives around. So I ask myself, "Is it possible for me to weigh 117 pounds again?" Or am I stuck with the belief that all women at the age of fifty-one tend to gain weight, and have a hard time losing it. Remember, we are all creative beings. Could it be possible to change my weight with my thoughts? Could this just be a belief that I have adopted? What about other issues in our lives? Is it as simple as changing a few thoughts? As I sit here this morning, the angel Metatron comes through loud and clear with the answer.

The following is a channeling session with Metatron as he brings his wisdom to us with a stern but loving heart.

Channeling Metatron: The Gatekeeper To Our Thoughts

A new day dawns; it is time to come from your rest and enter the world of daily tasks. As you deal with the people, places and situations in this day, you always have a choice. It is time for all of mankind to be responsible for what they think, for thoughts are "things," and what you think you will create and bring forth. I am here to let you know that you can make the change right now. You can take a stand for your highest good, knowing that I am by your side helping you all the way. Stop right now and scan your thoughts. What are you thinking at this very moment? Is the cup half full or half empty? Do you truly want to create the thoughts that you are thinking? Free will is part of your journey here on earth. So once again I say you have a choice. Believe in yourself and your power to bring good. Know that you are only a step away from the perfection that is your God-given birthright. Where is it that you truly want to dwell? So I ask that in this very moment that you become aware of your thoughts, and choose them wisely, for they are truly the key to your happiness and fulfillment here on earth.

Metatron Guides Me

As I read the information that has been channeled this morning, I can truly see where I want to go. I know that each day is special, and may hold the key to all the goodness that is to come in the future. I ask Metatron to come along with me on my journey and to whisper in my ear when my thoughts start to stray, as he reminds me that I always have a choice. Call upon Metatron to guide you towards a bright and prosperous future. As your goals start to manifest, remember that although a thought is not an object that you can hold in your hand, it is still a form of energy that will manifest, for we are truly the creators of our destiny.

Forever And Always

My thoughts this morning start to flow, and my dear husband, Walter comes to mind. He has been gone for over twenty-three years, and I still remember his laugh, and his kind and generous nature. He comes to me from time to time, and always watches over our daughter, Cristina Michelle. I feel compelled to write this poem for him, and to let him know that he was one of the many "treasures" in my life.

In God's Arms

Walter, I see you as clear as can be
Your smile and your humor for heaven to see
Your kindness and love
Your laughter so deep
Your curly dark hair
The size of your feet

Your love for me cherished
Your support such a gift
For you were so special
With words that uplift

I know you're in heaven
No doubt in my mind
In God's arms you landed
In God's arms so kind

Your daughter she knows you
I made sure of that
Her father, dear father
In a special habitat

The love that you send her
The gifts from above
The times that I prayed
Yes, you heard me, my love

Not a moment too soon
For you came where we dwell
So close to us Walter
Good fortune you sell

I feel you, dear husband
In this very day
I feel you, dear husband
In the words that you say

In God's arms you landed, I know this is true
In God's arms you landed, with much work to do
So we wait for your gifts, my husband, my friend
The gifts from the heavens, the gifts never end

So thankful you stayed in spirit, my dear
A husband in heaven who will always be near

A Gift From Her Father

At the age of twenty five my beautiful daughter, Cristina was about to graduate from college. I have watched her over the past five years as she has blossomed into a loving and talented young woman. Her gifts are many, and she is about to receive a degree in Visual Arts from Pine Manor College in Chestnut Hill, Massachusetts. Her photography is unique. She has a true eye for color, and a great sense of depth perception. She has received several awards for her artistic photos, and she has presented her work at several art shows at the college. There were times when I wondered what it would have been like if her father Walter were still alive to share our daughter's success. My question on this was answered, however, the day she graduated. I had been planning all week for Cristina's graduation, buying just the right gift, as well as inviting friends and family to the graduation. I had also made plans to take everyone out for dinner to celebrate. The graduation would be outside on the Pine Manor Campus, and the tents were already set up the day I picked up

Cristina's cap and gown. It was then that I heard the weather report for that Sunday. Heavy rain was predicted starting the night before, and continuing through the entire day. As I drove home from the school, I prayed that the weather man was wrong. I had pictured the graduation on the beautiful historic grounds with the sun shining, and the many pictures I would take of Cristina and her college friends. As the day grew closer the weather report hadn't changed. The students would still have to walk from the school to the field where the tents were set up. They would get soaked, and so would everyone else trying to make their way over to the commencement ceremony.

It was Saturday night, and as I lay in bed, I felt a nudge as if the angels were telling me that I had a visitor in the room. I felt a presence, and when I asked who it was my dear husband, Walter spoke. He told me that he would take care of everything, and that the day would be a true gift from him to Cristina. I told him that if he could only hold off the rain until we went to dinner it would be the best gift he could ever give her. I fell off to sleep that night, and felt positive that Walter would come through with his promise. Lo and behold, I woke up the next day and there wasn't a drop of water on the ground. When we left the house for the graduation the sun came out a few times, and then clouds would come but it never rained. Not a drop! The ceremony was a success, and the pictures I got of Cristina were beautiful. Her boyfriend Marc was there, and took pictures of the two of us, and also the friends and family who attended.

We left after the ceremony and went to dinner, and as we were coming out of the restaurant, it started to rain. Now tell me that isn't a sign. Walter had somehow held off the rain for his daughter. What an incredible and credible gift! As Cristina and I walked towards the school after the graduation, I told her about her father and the gift she had received from him. She smiled, and we hugged knowing that Walter was there with us the whole time. Thank you, my love, for your gracious gift from up above. One other thing that I found rather amusing was that the weather man on t.v. that night couldn't quite explain how the rains had held off in a certain part of Chestnut Hill that day! If you would like to see some of my daughter's work, please feel free to go to her website, *geminess.com*. Both her father and I are very proud of her.

My channeling session with my husband goes as follows:

A Message From Walter

A deep sense of serenity is present here, and the energy that I feel is loving and supportive. There is no need for competition, for we all know who we are and enjoy watching as we grow together in harmony. To be here, and to feel what I feel, is a gift beyond all gifts. I know you will like it here, and when the time comes I will make sure that you get the "grand" tour.

A Message From Aneal And The Goddess Energy

It is so appropriate that the angel Anael came to me at this time.

I had just finished writing the poem, and asked if any other angels wanted to come through today, and there she was. After the passing of my dear husband, I felt lost, and at times very frightened. I had a three year old daughter to raise, and all the responsibilities that we had held as a couple. My life changed very quickly the night that Walter passed. The learning had just begun. As I sit here today and think back on the past twenty-three years, I have truly blossomed into a woman who knows herself better than I could have ever imagined. The departure of my husband was a test, one that I would eventually pass, and once I did, I would see that there was a light at the end of the tunnel. I had grown into a more self-sufficient and confident woman. This, to me, is truly a gift, and one I hope that every one of us can achieve in our lives. As I channel Anael this warm summer morning, she reminds me of this power, and she brings me the strength to "grow" further on my journey here in "Earth School."

Aneal brings prosperity and growth to those who are willing to find out who they "truly" are. Often times we are frightened to look too deep in fear of what we may discover. What Anael brings us is not only the courage but the determination so that we can fulfill our creative natures, and allow ourselves to be "All that we can be."

Channeling Anael Who Ushers In The Goddess

Your beauty surrounds you. I see it well. You are starting to blossom in ways that you never imagined. Your quest for a better way of life is evident, and I am willing to come to help you on this quest. The color orange is very important at this time. You must use this color to bring the energies forth, and for these stagnant energies to clear and become whole. There is so much to learn, and I am here to show you the way. You are a powerful spirit who has come here to make a difference. So let it be, and let it unfold. Allow this energy to surface in all its glory. You can now stand on your own two feet and take charge. Your body, mind, and soul connect and work as one. There is no separation, for you are a divine light on the earth plane. Destiny has stepped in and created your evolution. All has happened for a reason and a purpose. Trust and have faith in yourself. Prosperity is the outcome. Your boundaries are set, and you know where you are going. Without doubt and fear, allow this energy to flow through you. Bathe in the color orange. Allow this color to nourish and enliven all of your senses. You have tapped into this creative power at this time for a reason. Harness this now; move forward with conviction. For you are the goddess, and the goddess is all loving as she encompasses the powers of integrity and love. Take the step now and move forward, for I am supporting and guiding you, and praising you as you make your way on the path that you came here to follow.

Goddess Complete

The feminine energy born in this day
The feminine energy flows in a way

That's loving, and strong, and so very sweet
The feminine energy, the Goddess complete

A strength that is born from a soft, gentle place
A strength that is powerful with kindness and grace
The Goddess, the Goddess a true beauty I say
The Goddess, the Goddess in work and at play

A beacon of light for all to behold
A painting in progress that starts to unfold
Whose charity and love she encompasses all
The voice of the Goddess is never too small

For her power encompasses those she will love
The Goddess, the Goddess from heaven above
So I invite you to bring forth the Goddess in you
Allow her to flourish for there are so few

Who call forth her power in this very day
So call forth this power and do not delay
The beauty, the beauty the Goddess unfolds
As the story continues for all to behold

The Angel Abundantia Goddess Supreme

Your truth is my truth, and through this, prosperity reins. By allowing yourself love, and being devoted to your spirit's purpose here on earth, prosperity is inevitable. I must congratulate you now, for you have come "full circle." You have let go of all the misconceptions about who you truly are, and you are now willing to push through the maze. You hold your head high, and you are full of anticipation for a future that is bright. Prosperity is yours, embrace this gift, and watch as your life moves forward in ways that *you may have never imagined. With blessings I watch, as it all unfolds with great perfection, for what is the Goddess but the true essence of this.*

Chamuel Who Is Full Of Admiration

This morning as I complete my channeling session with Anael, I am compelled to listen to the sweet and gentle voice of Chamuel. She is soft, and loving, and the energies that flow from her lips are supportive and nurturing. She has a deep desire to bring prosperity to all who choose to listen, and she invites us to allow the love from others to enter and surround our very soul.

These Are Her Words

It is time for all of mankind to cherish and admire one another. There is no room for excuses. I promise that the gifts that will come are certainly more important than the separation that you put between one another. As you work and live your daily lives with other fellow human beings, it is time that you honor them and yourself. The gifts that follow are worth every bit of your time and effort. The energies multiply, and your commitment grows. Your accomplishments begin to unfold, and now is the time to show your adoration for all involved. Whether it is in your work or your personal life it is time, to put aside that which holds you back. Admire those around you, for they are a mirror of who you are. The lessons here are not to judge, but to look deep within, and see the true lesson. For each and every one of us comes to earth as a "player" and the "big picture" will be revealed if you go beyond the ego, and admire each and everyone of your fellow human beings for their part in the play. As we admire so we are admired, and so the cycle continues to flow in the direction that it was intended. I am the angel of adoration. I bring the energies of prosperity and devotion. Invite me into your life, and you will prosper in ways that you could never imagine, for what is prosperity but understanding. Those who learn the lessons are the ones who will truly prosper.

As I end my channeling today, I am delighted by the commitment and the love of spirit on the other side. They have come to guide us, and it seems that no matter what we do, they are truly committed to helping us understand what our purpose is on earth. I feel a deep sense of gratitude and love for them, and want them to know that I will continue on my path with their help. I feel honored to be part of their work, and will do my best to pass on this gift to all who come my way.

Once Again Nathaniel Comes Through With His Message

In many of my readings over the years, the angel Nathaniel has brought his energy and warmth to clients who have been ready to move forward in their lives. He is there to support them on their journey, and to help them transform the old into the new. His energy is positive, and like fire itself, catches on quickly. Movement is evident when Nathaniel comes through, and his message is welcomed and appreciated. Today I have had the pleasure of a channeling session with Nathaniel. I hope you enjoy the message he has for you.

A stand must be taken. Your power is available in ways that you may never have imagined. Movement is evident now, and you must open yourself to all of the possibilities. As humans, you often stop and have to question everyone and everything that crosses your path. You are wasting time. This moment is what you have been waiting for. Allow this energy to usher you to higher levels of consciousness. Release all doubts, and fears, for they will only hold you back. I will bring you all that you need to move forward. Call upon me as the opportunities multiply. You are in a very special place in your life. Transformation abounds, and it is time to make the move. The fiery warmth that I place around you will help you to move in ways that are freeing. Listen to your gut. Trust that feeling that is pushing you forward. This is not your imagination, but the truth and the "truth will set you free." I am here, for all you have to do is call upon me, and allow me to thrust you to the next level. You are not alone, for spirit is guiding you. Feel the energy, for this is your gift, and can be used to smooth your way. Take a deep breath now, release that which is holding you back. As the energy heats up, you will delight in the outcome. Your transformation has begun, and you have much to look forward to in the days ahead.

I have often felt the fiery warmth of Nathaniel in my life. I know that feeling of movement. The kind of feeling you just can't ignore. There have been times when I have allowed him to do his work, and other times when I have resisted out of fear. I now know that it is much easier to let go of the doubt and allow this powerful and loving energy guide me to the next step in my life. Always with kindness and compassion, Nathaniel comes to bring us to the next level.

Lessons From The Universe

The universe is a complex and extremely wonderful force. So many things affect us, and one of these forces comes from planetary influences. Since we are made up of energy, the forces around us can affect us in many ways. One example of this is in Applied Kinesiology where, through a series of muscle testing procedures, our body will tell us exactly what we need and don't need. Our energy is always changing, and these forces around us are working in ways that most of us aren't even aware. Many methods of holistic healing such as Reiki, Therapeutic Touch, Acupuncture, Massage, Hypnosis, and EFT (emotional freedom technique) just to name a few are all techniques to balance and heal our energy fields. Keeping this concept in mind, I would like to talk about another force that has a great deal of impact on who we are as humans. I have always felt that everything that is on this earth plane and beyond is a creation of God. He has given us everything we need. The planets and the solar system are two very important components that truly do have an affect on our lives. Like a blueprint, these forces can guide us and help us in many ways. This includes not only the birth sign we are born under, but also the other placements in our charts that at certain times are energized by planetary influences. Just think about how you feel sometimes when the moon is full. Many seem to feel their aliments more, and animals start to act a bit peculiar. The tides are affected, and so is the water table in our bodies. Since we are 75% water, this is a time when our moods are heightened and sometimes tempers flare. So in understanding this, we can look further into the planetary influences that affect us.

As I am writing this, the planet Mercury is about to go retrograde in a couple of days. I would like to make mention of the planet of communication and how it affects us. For those of you who are familiar with Mercury, you already know that it is the planet of "communication." The energy that Mercury exhibits is usually high and almost a bit nervous. When a retrograde takes place, this energy will slow, and things that normally would run smoothly or with some sort of ease tend to go a bit "haywire." In my readings, I often channel the angel, Uzziel right around the time Mercury is about to slow down in the sky. At these times, I must stop and let my client know that this is just a "resting period" and that Uzziel is here to tell them to have faith, knowing that right around the corner movement is evident, and a return to prosperity is certain. Uzziel also comes to let them know that although this is a resting period of sorts, it is also a time of re-evaluation. The universe is giving us a time when we can pull back and re-examine our lives. We have the opportunity to finetune our goals, and go within to capture the essence of our commitment here on earth. In many ways, Mercury retrograde can be a gift. A time to learn patience, and a time to re do the things in our lives that need some tender loving care. For approximately three weeks, we are given a "great" opportunity to "tweak" our goals and plan for the future. As the planets' energy slows, so does our own energy, and at times like this we are reminded that "rest" is important, and taking care of our bodies is a must. Balancing the energies of Mercury retrograde and learning to use this energy wisely truly is an opportunity for growth. Uzziel comes to us this morning with his point of view.

Channeling Uzziel: A Commitment To Faith

It is time to release the struggle. Having faith and trust is the key. I am here to guide you, and let you know that by having this faith you will come out the winner. It is time to stop and put aside all of your fears and apprehensions. Relax, and know that you are being guided. It is time for you to pull back, and to stop pushing so hard. Now is the time to go within. What is it that you truly want to create in your life? Are your goals truly your focus? Or are they something that you think you must accomplish for someone else? These are the questions that you must ask yourself. Prosperity is there for you. It is all about divine timing. Having trust and faith will guide you there easily and effortlessly. The choice is yours. Forcing the situation will only block the progress. Work with the energies at hand. I have full confidence in you, and so you must trust your feelings at this time. Learn to take a deep breath, and feel the energy surge that comes from relaxation. Now is the time to plan for your future. It is time to lay the foundation for things to come. So I say that you must stop and be calm for only then will the movement come. Gently move with this energy now, as you allow it to usher you on your path. Call upon me for guidance, and once again I say have faith. Kick out all doubts and fears. This is a resting period that is truly needed. Collect the knowledge, for it is power, and when the time is right action will take place in your life. Your hard work will be rewarded as the new energies support you, and help you to reach your highest goals.

Pink

Love & Unfolding Devotion

©2006 Mikki Cully

A CHANNELING FROM GALGALIEL: A SOUL MATE CONNECTION

Galgaliel brings forth the energies of the "Soul Mate" connection.

The beautiful colors that are present in this vibration are purples, greens, and pinks. Two beautiful souls brought together out of a commitment, and deep love for one another; our soulmates are here on earth to help and guide us along the way. The pure essence of love is present whenever the soulmate connection is made, and often this connection is the "One" very special love of our lives. Galgaliel comes today to bring us the purest and most loving information in regard to our soulmate connections. He brings us the understanding that accompanies this powerful and loving vibration in our lives.

It is with great pleasure that I bring this information to you. The universe is full of love. Your soulmate brings this love to you in many ways. The feelings that inspire you from your soulmate are rich and all-encompassing. Your desire or pull is quite different from other relationships. With great love in your heart you gravitate towards one another in a dance that is sensual and deep. I now pose this question to you. What purpose does your soulmate relationship serve? How do you affect one another? Often times you think that this "special love" must be perfect, and that the only feelings that are to be experienced are love and joy. To a point this is true, but then the learning must start to take place. This is the true purpose of the soulmate connection. Growth is all important, and the goal for your connection is to enrich and nourish, as well as to teach and guide one another. Two souls in heaven who commit to one another before birth. Lessons set ahead of time. How will you receive these lessons? Will you gracefully allow them into your life? Or will you run from them and hide for fear of what may come? The soulmate relationship is full of purpose. The love that emanates from these two souls is often deep and sometimes turbulent. In a perfect world these two souls enjoy the dimensions of every emotion that is known to man. So I say to you in this new day that the soulmate connection in your life is to be cherished and nurtured and appreciated, for the learning must be gradual and accepted. Do not judge the feelings that are present, but take the lesson that was given with love from your soulmate. Learn, grow, and accept this love and remember why you were attracted and what brought you together in the first place. Allow this connection to guide you on your path, without allowing ego to get in the way. Thank your soulmate for the input that has helped you to become the person you are today. As your love and appreciation are directed towards this spiritual connection so you shall receive this vibration of love back towards you. Stay on purpose. Allow your soulmate to bring forth the lessons that you came here to learn. Cherish and nurture your soul mate connection for it was meant to be.

My Soulmate

Your smile so warm, a pull I feel
Your lips so sweet and tender
I think of you both day and night
A gift that I must render

I know that you are here for me
Deep down inside my soul
From heaven it was set in stone
The lover, teacher role

We seem to know each other's thoughts
It feels so right, so true
We are as one at times I feel
We have so much to do

The learning it begins to flow
The test has now begun
Our love so deep, our laughter strong
The times of joy and fun

A mixture now of both I see
We share our love on earth
As I allow you in to teach
A decision made at birth

The lessons they will help us grow
Our purpose we will serve
To bring the love that's always there
This is the learning curve

So I invite you soulmate
To spend your life with me
In all the ways that matter
With love and joy the key

To learning all the lessons
That we share with one another
While keeping love alive a must
For I will have no other

Your love is all I need to see
That heaven up above
Has made this divine connection
Such a deep and special love

Bringing Joy To The World

Joy is a strong and wonderful feeling that comes from our hearts. Certainly a part of happiness, joy fills us with a sense of "well being." Although joy is always present, we seem to get "caught up" in our daily routine and forget to incorporate these feelings into our daily lives. The angel, Ramaela, has come to bring us her views on joy and to transform our views on this precious gift.

Channeling Ramaela Who Brings Joy To All

Rejoice, Rejoice, for joy is everywhere. Stop for a moment and look around you. Are God's gifts not present? Is this not joy? The vivid blue sky, the fluffy white clouds, the very earth that you stand on. How lucky to be part of it all. Joy is there. So very present. Again, I ask you to stop. Look around. The sweet air that fills your lungs and keeps you alive. The flower that has bloomed in your front yard. The colors so vivid so alive. Your eyes see, and your heart feels the joy. Your pet as it lies on the sofa, so warm, and tender is its love for you. Is this not joy? The kindness in your lover's eyes. The delightful smell of food cooking on the stove. The tender kiss of a loved one, as they return home. Children laughing, a baby's cry. Spending the day with a good friend. A kind word from a stranger. Is this not joy? For joy is everywhere if one takes the time to stop, and allow it to saturate the five senses. I say that you alone are joy and that joy is present in this very moment. So call upon me often, for I am Ramaela who brings joy to all who welcome it in. Please know that I am always ready to transform your sadness into joy for life is truly joy in the making. Open your hearts to the joy that is waiting to enter for it is free and always available to you.

Ramela's Joy

I feel the joy so clear so kind
It wants to be with me
For what is joy but a gift from God?
For all the world to see

A gentle hand on my shoulder lie
From a loved one in my life
The joy it flows, the joy it flows
I've put aside the fight
For I am joy and joy is me
Now and forever more

The joy it flows the joy it flows
So open up the door

So much to touch so much to taste
The joy is everywhere
I feel the joy in your sweet smile
Your tending loving care

So let's rejoice in this new day
The joy I feel I see
The joy that comes into my heart
The joy it sets me free

So I invite you now to stop
And feel the joy so near
It starts with you so let it flow
No time for doubt or fear

For joy is what will bring you hope
For all the world to see
And so the joy it flows through you
Transforming as can be

It is important that we acknowledge the joy that surrounds us. Like the cup half full, it will enliven our spirits, and move us forward in a positive and healing way.

Before I end this channeling session, I feel the presence of my Guardian Angel. Her name is Sonata, and she has a very special message to share with all of you today.

Sonata Spreads Her Joy

Please send your love and light out into the world today, and tomorrow, as well, for it is needed to bring awareness to the energies that are lost. Your light will embrace this energy and bring clarity. You are the guiding light in this new day, and the love that emanates will heal and soothe an aching society. Spread the word now, and let others know of your intentions. Each new day is an opportunity to shine your light. Your heart will fill, and joy and healing will be the outcome.

Writing To The Angels

The angels are here for us whenever we are open and ready for their help. Often times we have questions that are of a personal nature, and we feel that we must hold our emotions in for fear of embarrassment. We all want to be understood, but often we just don't know the right way to go about it. Here is a wonderful technique for writing to the angels and getting answers.

Make sure you have a pen in hand and as much paper as you need!
1. First, I suggest you find a cozy spot to rest.

2. Burning a lovely candle nearby is a wonderful gift to the angels and shows them that you are calling them forth. I suggest a white or pastel candle. The energy is light and the angels love soft colors.

3. Now, take a deep breath in slowly through your nose and out through your mouth. This is a cleansing breath, and will clear the channel for the angels to do their work. Practice this three to four times until you feel relaxed.

4. Feel your body's connection to the chair or surface where you are sitting. If you are sitting on the floor, feel your body connecting to the earth below. This is a grounding technique, and will help with the process.

5. Close your eyes, and picture what your angel might look like. You will start to feel a presence around you. Don't worry about a specific experience; just know that your angel is here to help.

6. At the top of your paper, put the date.

7. Next, think of your angel and remember they are like a close friend. Ask for your angel's guidance in this matter, and then start writing whatever it is that you need help with.

8. When you are finished, sign the letter with love and appreciation.

9. Put the letter in an envelope, and on the front address it to your angel.

10. A special name may come to you; feel free to write this name down on the envelope. Angels come to us with many names and faces.

11. Now find a place to put your angel letter. Some like to put the letter under their pillows. Others will put the letter in their favorite spot around the house. This is up to you. Go with what feels right inside.

12. You will receive answers now in many forms. The angels are doing their work, and you can feel confident that an answer will come. I have

found that when I do this exercise people, places, and situations come to guide and help me. A book will stand out or someone will say a word or two, and a light will go off inside of me. Other times I have received phone calls or mail that would help me with my search; remember the old proverb from the Bible "seek and ye shall find." Being open is the key. Let your angels show you the way, and always remember to trust your gut feeling as the answers flow down to you.

Here are several other ways to connect with our heavenly friends.

Bringing Forth The Angels On A Daily Basis

Take several deep cleansing breaths. This is important for grounding. Think of your situation or problem and then when you are ready be open to allowing angelic energy in to help. The words I often use are "my dear sweet angels, I invite you in at this time to guide me and help me with this problem _____. You fill in the blank. It always amazes me because within a short period of time, I will receive some sort of answer from them, whether it's a conversation with a stranger, a song on the radio or mail from that day. Sometimes I have to trust and wait a few days, but the answer always appears. The key is to be open and trust.

Dream Angels

This is another process that seems to work very well. I sit down before going to bed and write out a question and direct it to the angels, loved ones and benevolent beings on the other side. I put it under my pillow, and before going to sleep I once again invite them in to help me solve the problem. Dreams may bring the answer but often I come across a solution the next day. Divine timing does have a lot to do with this, of course, and sometimes we have to wait for the answer. Do not despair for even if the answer comes in bits and pieces, it will present itself.

THE ANGEL ZADKIEL: ANSWERING OUR PRAYERS

You have not been forgotten for your prayers are affirmations, and like shooting stars, they fly up towards the heavens. As they are caught they are read, and put into the order of "divine timing." This, of course, is a lesson in patience, for when the time is right your prayers will be answered for your highest good. You must take a deep breath now and relax, for I have not forgotten your "heart's desire." Make a conscious effort to put aside that which is no longer needed, for I will help you to clear out the old so the new can bring about the answered prayer that is about to come your way. This is a process of sorts, but a divine process indeed. This only requires a bit of trust and faith, knowing that your angels are taking care of all of your needs now and in the future. Watch as your prayers are answered, and continue to claim what is yours, for you are truly a blessing to work with, as I will continue to guide you each and every step of the way. Remember to affirm:

<u>Everything is in a Divine and Perfect order right now!</u>

These angels have a special fondness in their heart for their special sign. Call upon them for guidance for they understand the needs and desires of your birth sign.

Aries	(March)	Machidiel
Taurus	(April)	Asmodel
Gemini	(May)	Ambriel
Cancer	(June)	Muriel
Leo	(July)	Verchiel
Virgo	(August)	Hamaliel
Libra	(September)	Uriel
Scorpio	(October)	Barbiel
Sagittarius	(November)	Adnachel
Capricorn	(December)	Hanael
Aquarius	(January)	Gabriel
Pisces	(February)	Barchel

There is also a special angel for each day of the week. Whichever day you were born on, this angel will be part of your journey.

Monday's Angel

The Archangel Gabriel has been assigned to the child who is born on Monday. Gabriel embraces life, and all the many facets of it. He loves to raise your spirits, and pull you up when life seems to be throwing you a curve. He projects all that is good, and good fortune is always in his message. He is diligent in delivering the gifts that God so wants to bestow upon us and is very majestic and powerful. Gabriel helps us to remember our purpose here on earth, and will go to great lengths to help us reach our goals. *Set your goals high and believe in yourself for this will bring about your success.* Call upon Gabriel to help you with your daily tasks for he is more than willing to assist you. His main goal is to create emotional balance around you, and he is associated with the color peach, as well as the flower scents of jasmine, rose and sandalwood. Crystals and citrine are his favorite semi-precious gems. He has much to teach us about our role here on earth. Call upon him often for he sits gently on your shoulder.

Tuesday's Angel

Camael is the angel for Tuesday. Camael is the "angel of self love" and divine justice is this angel's calling. You will find Camael in all places of worship, and the ocean is a perfect dwelling for Camael to spend time. To love oneself as well as others is the lesson that this angel teaches, and Camael is called upon in situations where love has gone or is about to bloom. *To give and receive love is one of the most important gifts on earth.* This angel is in the celestial order of seraphim, and the color saffron will attract this loving angel. Mars is the governing planet, and personal power and love along with self-expression are this angel's goals. Ylang Ylang, bergamot, and vetivert will attract Cameal, and sunstone, yellow citrine and quartz are the gems that call Cameal forth. Working on self-confidence is of utmost important to Tuesday's angel, so allow Cameal to show you the way. The love that emanates from Cameal is all-encompassing so call upon this angel whenever you feel a lack of love in your life.

Wednesday's Angel

The Archangel Raphael is here for Wednesday's child. Healing is Raphael's favorite pastime as he surrounds his children with his large emerald wings. He is one of the angels who ushers healing into our lives. Some of Raphael's best work is done in hospitals, and in places where people are trying to heal. He asks that you place your thoughts on beauty, health and fitness for he will guide you on the path to "perfect health." Raphael believes that the body is a "temple" and that the foods, thoughts, and the environment we live in all affect this wonderful domain. If you are feeling ill or fatigued, just close your eyes and ask for Raphael's healing touch. Soon you will be energized, and your health will improve. He watches over our loved ones when they are ill, as well as sharing his love for us at all times. Ask for Raphael's help if you have a health concern or just want to get in shape. He will put the right people, places, and situations in front of you. Pink and green are his favorite colors, and he is ruled by the planet Mercury. Touch is very important to Raphael, so allow him to come with his soothing touch and make a difference in your life today. *Forgive those who have scorned you, for forgiveness brings healing.* Call upon Raphael when your energy is low or when you aren't feeling well. He will swoop down and surround you with his beautiful emerald wings, healing all of those who ask for his help.

Thursday's Angel

Metatron is the angel of "thought." Thursday is governed by this angel, and Metatron is there both day and night, as he watches over our thoughts. Always willing to bring clarity to a situation, Metatron displays a great wealth of knowledge. *Thoughts are things, and the flow of your thoughts creates your reality.* Metatron is very powerful, and he will help us to change our negative thoughts into positive ones. He will help to clear your mind and show you the truth. Many goals can be accomplished with the help of Metatron, so call upon this angel often for guidance and support. Lapis Blue is his favorite color, and will attract him as well as the scents myrrh and chamomile. Aquamarine and turquoise are his favorite crystals. Self- expression is his specialty, so feel free to contact him often for all of your projects and endeavors. He will direct you into "right thinking" and you will see your life unfold in a positive and uplifting way.

Friday's Angel

Uriel is a very special Archangel. Salvation is this angel's purpose, and he seeks to help those who are ready to turn their lives over to a higher power. The light of God shines brightly around Uriel, and the sun is one of his favorite planets. He travels fast and will arrive at one's beck and call. He is like the sun and the warmth that it projects, and all that he touches will shine. If life's pressures are getting you down, it is time to call upon Uriel for emotional support. He will assist you in closing one door and opening another. He supports positive changes in your life. *Please call upon me often for it is my duty and pleasure to assist you.* Stability will reign, and a sense of well-being will return. Uriel is "God's burning flame," as he shines brightly for all of those who call upon his divine presence. The third eye is the chakra in which Uriel resides, and the colors red and yellow are what draw him close. Allow Uriel to come into your life today, and watch the sun start to shine where darkness once reigned.

Saturday's Angel

Cassiel watches over those of you born on Saturday. Being the "Angel of Temperance," Cassiel will boost your creative power, and put you in touch with the true power of your being. What do you desire most in your life? Once you know this, Cassiel will be happy to guide you in attaining your goals. The physical is also part of Cassiel's calling, and this Archangel has no trouble adding energy and zest to your life. Feeling low? Call upon Cassiel to lift you both mentally and physically. Nature is also a place that Cassiel respects and loves. A walk on the beach, in the forest or on a nature trail, these are some of Cassiel's favorite places. Are you grateful for all that you have in your life? Cassiel will shed many blessings on those who are aware of what they already have. *Those who already know what they have are truly blessed.* So count your blessings daily, and watch Cassiel bring forth more than you ever imagined. Churches and sacred dwellings are also favorite places, and gold, violet, and white are the colors in which Cassiel delights. Lavender, rosewood, and frankincense are the scents he adores, and diamonds, as well as amethys, are his favorite gems. Flowers will also bring forth this angel, and prayers are appreciated and welcome in his presence. Call upon the energy of Cassiel for all creative endeavors, and I'm sure you will be delighted with the outcome!

Sunday's Angel

Born on the Sabbath Day? Michael the Archangel is watching over you. Protection is his goal, and he diligently watches over you as well as the ones you love. He is the warrior and protector who guards the gates of heaven. He will protect you on your path to enlightenment and will make sure that you are guided along the way. He has quite an appetite for spiritual knowledge and will come to the aid of all those on a quest for spiritual growth. Are you feeling a bit stagnant lately? Does your personal growth seem to be diminishing? Call upon Archangel Michael to rekindle the flame. He will support and guide your spiritual growth, and make sure you stay on the right path. Trust in him, and know he is always around you. *I am honored to watch over the people of the earth.* His power and strength are immense, and his mighty presence is felt by all who choose to call upon his divine nature. He is very responsible and doesn't take his responsibilities lightly. He is here to fulfill our spiritual needs, and patchouli, cedar wood, and myrrh are his favorite scents. He teaches us to stand up for all that we are, and hematite, tiger's eye and bloodstone are the gems in which he delights. Crimson is his favorite color, and the root chakra is where he dwells. Call upon this heavenly protector for your needs. He will never let you down.

The angels are always available to us. They are here to guide, and help us here on earth. Since free will is a part of life, the angels come especially when we invite them in. It's time to look, and see where the angels can come and help you. Either by using your birth angel, golden angel, the day you were born angel, or calling forth angelic energy in general, the angels are available and truly willing to support and help us both night and day.

Angelic Goals

A friend who comes from up above
With goals that are so many
To guide and show us all the way
A friend with goals so many
"Free will, Free will," the angels say

We know you must be ready
To call upon and ask for help
The angels strong and steady

To help us through our darkest hour
To help with joy and peace
Since life brings both, they help us now
So we must just release

The fear and doubt that often comes
When trust is what we need
The angels come, they show us how
With love and grace, God speed

Down towards the earth they spread their wings
They know just where to go
Your house, my house, the girl next door
Whenever the need is to grow

For faith and trust is what we learn
From their unconditional love
A gift from heaven, a special friend
Like wings upon a dove

They soar above our planet now
For needed they truly are
The wars, the hate, so unlike love
The angels near and far

So let them in and let them do
The work they do with love
For angels they are everywhere
A gift from God above

This afternoon the angel, Uriel has come through with some very important information for all of us.

Channeling Uriel

What is it that you are committed to in this lifetime? What are your hopes and dreams for the future? The healing is starting to take place, yet many of you are following the wrong path. It is time to stop and ask the question, "What makes me feel alive? What is it that I am drawn to do?" I have come to let you know that the answer is there for you if you take the time to know yourself. I bring you the courage to look deep inside and then venture out into the world. So many light workers are needed. As humans, your capabilities are many. Stop restricting yourselves! There is no need to put restrictions on your talents. Listen to the voice inside that wants to come forth and make a difference. The old voices from the past are not the truth. It is your own inner voice that tells you what is real. I invite you to look at what is deep down inside. I ask that you allow me to help you bring it to the surface, allowing yourself to develop into the creative being that God intended you to be. Only you can start the process. Take some time now and ask the questions. Then allow the answers to come when the time is right. Many healing hands are being wasted. It is time for the earth to heal. You are part of that healing, so pick up your hands and use them to comfort and soothe your fellow human beings. You are not alone, and guidance is available if you just have the courage to ask. I promise you will not be disappointed.

Guardian Angel

Children near and children far
I am here to show you the way
I promise not to leave your side
I promise not to stray

My love for you so deep, so deep
I truly am committed
To showing you just who I am
An angel who is fitted

To know just who you are, my child
I know you oh so well
I feel the love so deep inside
For deep is where I dwell

I see your tears, I feel your joy
I sit upon your shoulder
My job is to protect and watch
In youth and when you're older

For always I will be with you
For age is just a number
So you can count upon me now
For you do not encumber

So whether it is day or night
I stand close by your side
A guardian forevermore
An angel here to guide

Channeling Ananchel In All Her Grace

Ananchel, I feel your love, your commitment, and your devotion to all who call upon you. As I have channeled your message many times, I always feel a sense of protection and warmth. Very much like a Guardian Angel, Ananchel is there for all of us. She brings the energies of kindness and love, but do not take that for signs of weakness, for Ananchel is strong in her convictions, and she is here to guide us and show us that honesty is the best policy. The following is a channeling session with Ananchel, in all her grace.

Show kindness and love towards all mankind. Shed light on that which is dark, by showing a helping hand. Come from your heart and let others see that you are here for a purpose. Tell them that everyday life is often full of obstacles but that the answers will come if they take the time to listen. I want to come to all of you and make a difference. My heart is filled with knowledge, and, at times, I feel as if I will burst. I ask that you open your hearts and minds to this knowledge, and allow me to feed and nourish you. So as you invite me in and share your goals and dreams with me, I will help to transform all that is for your highest good. This is the job of the angel of grace. For what is grace but a "pardon" from situations that are holding you back. Trust that there is a solution. Set your goals high, and look for the light that will lead you towards your goal. Never give up, for there is so much more than meets the eye. Your time has come. The transformation takes place. Grace surrounds you and shows you the way. Doubts and fears are replaced with gratitude and strength. Like a shadow that has been lifted, your pardon is here. Use this gift wisely. Be diligent about your goal. Know that I am with you, guiding you along the way. Call upon me often, for I am by your side. Excitement abounds; show all who come your way that it is possible. Let others feel your enthusiasm. For by sharing, you are passing on a gift, one that will dispel darkness into light for all the world to see.

Sending Angels To Loved Ones

Often when I hear of someone close who needs guidance and help, I will speak to the angels on his/her behalf. I have sent angelic energy to many situations knowing that the angels would follow suit, and help the other person in a special way. Once again, to do this all one has to do is the following: Think of the situation that needs healing or guidance, now take a few deep breaths and think of the person who needs angelic help. Picture them and say their name. Now you can call upon the angels to come in and shed light and healing on them. The angels always respect our "free will" so they come in a way that is nurturing and loving. Often, a friend will call and tell me that a solution appeared in a strange sort of way or that the problem felt smaller than before. I also like to use the "Light of God" prayer to encircle them and send them positive energy. The prayer goes as follows:

The light of God surrounds _____

The love of God unfolds _____

The power of God flows through _____

Wherever _____ is God and his angels are and all is well

Once I have said this, I send light in different colors for healing:

White light which pours down from the heavens as it heals and protects

Pink light for love and healing on an emotional level

Emerald Green light for physical healing

Deep Crimson light for energy and stamina

Purple light for enlightenment and protection

I have also put protection around loved ones by calling forth Archangel Michael, the Virgin Mary, and Archangel Raphael, the angel of healing. I am also a firm believer in Saint Anthony, and have always used his wonderful healing powers to guide a loved one home safely and to find missing items. The saints, like the angels, are part of the "realm" of friends that God has given us to call upon for guidance and support.

Channeling Sandlphon Who Ushers In Personal Power

Sandlphon's energy is hot and fiery, and catches on very quickly. As I sit with him this morning I feel the warmth and commitment that is emanating from his heart.

Connect with your soul. Slow down and go within. Learn to know who you are and your purpose. The strength that I bring you will guide you and show you the way. It is time to look deep inside without fear of what you will find. You are a pure and loving light, and fear will only hold you back. I bring you the personal power to move forward in all directions. I connect you with truth. It is time to put aside the old beliefs knowing that you have a divine purpose here on earth. It is time for you to come forth, as you show others your strength. They will bow down and support your efforts. Take charge of your life. Kick out that which holds you back. Power from your very being is struggling to come to the surface. There is no need for apprehension, for I sit on your shoulder and whisper in your ear. Power can be used for "goodness," and when you come from your heart, and from love, you will realize power is only truth. This truth shows you who you really are, and what you have come to do here on the earth plane. Delegate to others for in this way you show them their power, as well. A grand team of energies who know what is to be done. Trust in yourself, knowing that you and you alone can make the change. Take the first step, for as one door closes another opens. Have faith in the beautiful soul that was given to you at birth. This is your chance to connect with the part of yourself that has yearned for completion. Take my hand, and together we will walk along the path. As you become stronger, I will let go and watch from afar. I will continue to guide you on your quest for self-knowledge, and personal growth.

The Angel Shushienea: Purification On All Levels

Cleansing is an important part of our "life process." On a physical level our bodies try to cleanse on a daily basis. This is ongoing and a must if we are to stay healthy. The emotional self is also cleansed from time to time when we "purge" our emotions through such avenues as crying and verbal communication. Letting go of old beliefs can be a part of our spirits letting go and moving on. Through releasing and letting go of the old, the new, fresh and vital enter, and we can move forward on our journeys. Often you've heard the term that when one door closes, another one opens. This, too, is part of the cleansing process. Through cleansing our body, mind, and spirit, we can move to the next level of our process here on earth. Out of this purification there is a great sense of prosperity. Unlike a gift that one holds, this is felt deep down inside of us. Satisfaction and growth is the best way to describe this, and Shushienae, the angel of purity, has come to bring us her thoughts on the subject.

Channeling The Angel Of Purity

The cleansing process has begun. No need to turn back. Release, release, and allow the energies to flow as they cleanse your very soul. I promise that out of your willingness to "let go" a great gift will follow. You are about to embark on a journey. Allow this to unfold, as it brings you the clearing, and cleansing you need to go to the next level. I am with you, guiding you, and showing you the way. As I walk with you, allow me to bring you towards the life you so deserve. By releasing the old, and allowing the new to enter, you have made a wise decision. It is time, and so you must release. The process will start with the body, and the mind and spirit will follow. Drink the waters that are pure. Add the fruit of the lemon to clear the old stagnant energies that have accumulated. Eat the greens that God has provided, and the berries and seeds that the earth has grown just for you. Allow the old feelings to come to the surface. Be a gentle observer now, and as the feelings start to flow, allow them to purge and release. No need to grab on at this time. You are watching and then letting go. "Letting go is easy" becomes your daily mantra, and you will use these words often. It is time, so please do not resist. *The treasures that will come your way are many, and you will be guided and helped through the daily events in your life. Just commit yourself right now to the process, and the heavens will open with all the earthly and spirit help that is always available to you. Healing is the outcome. So the time is right for this gift to be bestowed upon you from the heavens. Open your arms wide now and accept the goodness. Willingness is all that is required.*

My Path Is Clear

To cleanse, to clear, in this new day
To cleanse, to clear, this is the way
To move forward now, the time is right
To release, let go, put aside the fight

So kick aside all doubt and fear
The angels are here to help, my dear
You're not alone, help's on its way
So cleanse, so clear, in this new day

For just around the corner, you'll see
Enlightenment comes, for it must be
So take the steps and close one door
Another opens, with joy in store

Trust and faith is all you need
Life fresh and new with this good deed
To help and support yourself right now
To cleanse, to clear, I'll show you how

It can be simple if you allow
The help that is there from up above
Angelic beings, so filled with love

So "congratulations" is in order, I see
The leap of faith, so meant to be
The grace that comes from an angel's love
The peace that follows from above

You've cleansed and so the journey goes
You have been cleansed from head to toe
So light and clear, your soul is free
For your newfound path was meant to be

Channeling Cerviel Who Brings Us Courage

It is time to be bold. It is time to pull together, and use the courage that lies dormant inside. You have the power, and must now have the willingness to call forth this energy. You have more pull than you think. As humans I see a group of souls who think little of themselves. They seem to fear their own personal development at times, and also have a hard time seeing who they truly are. I invite you to go deep inside, and ask the questions. Do not be afraid of the answers, for they will only bring you the joy you so deserve. Fear is just a human emotion. Please do not give it the energy to overpower you. Courage is the opposite, and today I bring this powerful yet loving energy to you. Take charge right now. Make the choices that you know are right in your heart. Do not hold back any longer. I have come to all of you in this new day to show you how. Stand tall and pull back your shoulders. Know who you are and your goodness. Speak from the truth, and allow others to feel that they are not alone. You will then spark the truth in your fellow man. Be the example that your children need. Show them that which is possible, and that courage prevails. My promise to you is that I will be by your side. Take the strength from my words if you feel tired and weak. I know who you are. I will pull you up, and courage will push you forward. Just take the first step now. Come towards me and fall into my arms, for I am Cerviel the angel of courage, and I will continue to be by your side. Like a mountain that is strong, and all enduring, so is the courage I bring to you.

One Friday Night

I am gathered now with several friends. It is time to make the choice. Shall we gossip or shall we send love, light and healing? This is so different from what most people normally do. I feel the energy as we hold hands. Our minds are one, and we are committed to bringing healing to the situation. Could our thoughts alone really make that much of a difference? Is it possible to stop the chatter and focus on a positive and loving outcome for all? The ego comes in and out, as we question once more. I feel the love in my heart, as well as in those around me, and I ask for the angels' guidance. It seems so simple, and yet the power that emanates from our intention is stronger than any verbal communication. As our intention grows, we feel as if we have become one, and, for a brief moment, it is euphoric. As humans, we yearn to make a difference, and often feel it must be done with something more tangible than thought. I have learned much over the years, as I continue to search for the truth. I have come to the conclusion that our thoughts are powerful, and what we send others, they feel. I myself feel it when others gossip about me, and my expression of this is that I lose the desire to see them and be their friends. We have the power to harm with words of slander or to heal with thoughts of love. What will you choose in this new day? I ask that you consider both avenues and make a choice. This doesn't make you good or bad, but one brings separation, and the other brings connection and love. The choice is yours. You decide.

"If you judge people, you have no time to love them."
— Mother Theresa

You Have A Friend

A friend drops by and brings the joy
The love within her heart

We've known them for a lifetime
We hope to never part

For many years we grew together
Our joy, our tears are one
Support and love is what you bring
The times of play and fun

Our words, they make a difference
They can make us smile indeed
Or how a word can cut us deep
It plants a different seed

For words can make a difference
We all know this is true
Some words they comfort deeply
Some words they make us blue

So, as your friend, I choose the words
That you will understand
I bring them to you with my heart
I hope you'll do the same

For thoughts and words they conquer
There is no need for blame
I love you now, my special friend
You mean so much to me

A love that comes so pure so true
Returned to you tenfold
A love that's pure and simple
A love that's fresh and bold
I listen now before I speak
For words will set one free
A friend who is devoted
Two souls so meant to be

Embrace each friend that comes your way
Their soul will feel your love
A love that comes from God himself
From heaven up above

And as my friend you're special
As special as can be
For love is what it's all about
And love will set us free

Yellow

Clarity

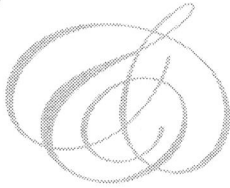

Gifts of Wisdom

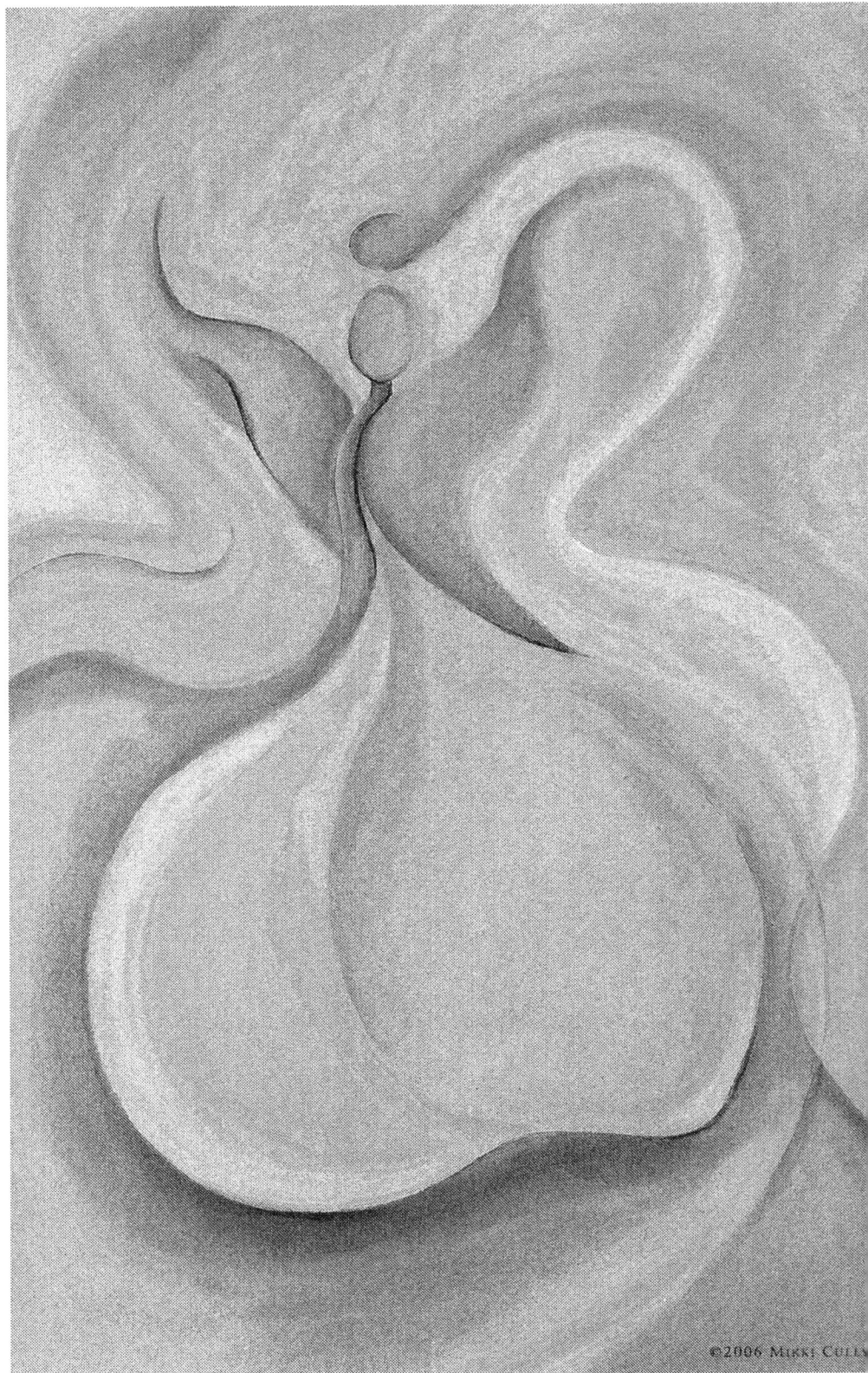

As I sit here this morning, I feel the presence of the angel Raziel, who is filled with enthusiasm, allowing me to channel these words of wisdom.

Channeling Raziel, Who Loves To Teach

It has come to my attention that many are avoiding the knowledge that will bring them to the next level in their spiritual growth. It is time to put aside the resistance now and move forward. The earth is moving at a quicker pace in these times, and much can be accomplished. Focus and put aside all apprehension. Start at the beginning if you must, and then move towards your goal. I am here, and ask that you call upon me, for I will guide you on your quest for greater knowledge. Ask the questions, and the answers will come. Listen to the voice that lies deep inside. Take the time to be quiet, for silence is of the outmost importance. Know that this movement in your life is inevitable. Try not to judge what is happening. Enjoy the new, and fresh, and vital energies that are entering. As if it were "meant to be," you will come across all that you need. Forge forward now, and push aside any obstacles that come your way. This is your growth cycle. This is a time when you will be able to "move mountains." Trust yourself, feel the power coming from that spot deep inside once more. Believe in yourself knowing that you always have a choice. Choose wisely, as divine love intervenes, and guides you, as you grow and learn. You are like a flower in bloom. Feed this beautiful flower, as you watch the vibrancy to which it transforms. This is spirit, your spirit. It is to be cherished and nurtured. Step out of your comfort zone now, and pursue that which answers your many questions. For knowledge is power and will bring about the transformation that you so desire.

All things are possible for me!

Herb Peterson

Back in the late 1980's I had the pleasure of meeting a spirit-filled, older man named Herb. He was a "palm" reader and a spiritual teacher, and his heart was full of compassion and love. A co-worker had told me about him and so I decided to make an appointment the following week. It was funny because I only met him the one time, but his words of wisdom had a deep and lasting affect on me. He was truly a "teacher" with a heart of gold, and as I sat with him that warm summer evening he began to reveal the many events of the past, present, and future. I had always been extremely curious about "things" that were beyond the veil, and so I was truly intrigued by his gift. As we sat together at his kitchen table, he proceeded to tell me about my personality, my heart's desires, the experiences that I had once had, and the ones to come. It was amazing because he didn't miss a detail. He told me I would be working with spirit, and that it would all unfold very easily and without effort. He told me about a healing that would take place around me, and how a man would come into my life who would be very supportive of my work. He talked about my emotional nature and how I could use my sensitivities to help others and how I would need to learn to focus these emotions for a "higher purpose." As I left that evening, he had left a lasting impression on me. I would never see Mr. Peterson again on this earth plane, for several years after our meeting he passed away, but when I think of him I feel as if I just left his kitchen table. I feel compelled to thank him for his guidance and devotion to others knowing that someday we will meet again.

Here is a tribute to you, Herb. I hope it brings a smile to your warm and loving heart.

The Hand of Fate

As time goes by, I see your face

So kind and oh, so true

Your guidance it will never leave

Embedded in my hand

The answers to the soul within

Understanding, acceptance and love

For I still feel your presence

On clouds from up above

You sat with me and showed me how

To see what wasn't clear

To fill myself with faith and love

"Let go" of doubt and fear

Remembering your words so soft

The hug so tight and kind

A tribute to Herb Peterson

In God's hands is where you'll find

His tender warmth his smile so bright

His commitment to what is true

So thank you, Mr. Peterson

There's no one quite like you

Herb's Words of Wisdom; A Channeled Message

From the moment I entered the light, I knew I was in the right place. The joy in my heart was immense, and the anticipation of what I was about to discover overwhelmed me. I was greeted by a feeling of unconditional love and acceptance. I have since then done some of my best work and feel that I have been surrounded with the kind of love that each and every one of you on the earth plane deserves. So I ask that you begin to open your heart now, and allow God's love to enter your soul for it is his biggest gift of all.

A Vacation With Spirit: Lily Dale, New York

In August of 2005, Preston and I took a trip to Lily Dale. For those of you who aren't familiar with this little town in upstate New York, it is a "camp" of sorts for the Spiritualist Church. A town that is full of love and devotion and especially "spirit-filled." I had first heard of Lily Dale sometime in June on the popular TV show, "Chronicle." As they described this quaint and serene little town, my desire to go there grew. Full of spirit and mediumship, the town of Lily Dale was to draw me towards its beautiful healing energy and its words of wisdom from beyond. The fact that I channel angelic energy and have been given the gift of mediumship was part of the desire to make the trip, so on August 8th, 2005 we headed towards the divine town of Lily Dale, New York. We would be staying at the "Angel Inn" which seemed so very appropriate, and, as we traveled towards our destination, I felt a sense that somehow I would fit right in. At one o'clock in the afternoon, we entered the gates. Literally, there is a gate! The only people who live in this serene little town by the lake are spiritualists, healers, and mediums.

The day was sunny and bright, and, as we drove towards the center of town, we could see all of the quaint little Victorian-style houses around us. The town green was right smack in the middle and behind the houses on one side was the lake. I could feel the peace and tranquility as I entered the gates. It was a little town separated from all of the rest of the world, and the energy was complex and at the same time very refreshing. As we took the corner, there at the top of the hill sat the "Angel Inn." A large white Victorian with a huge front porch and two angel statues placed on either side of the front steps.

The owner came out to greet us, and we entered the side door where we were taken up the stairs to the second floor. When we got to the top, I seemed to gravitate towards the room at the end of the hall. It was full of angels, and the colors were so "me." It was in a sunny corner of the house, and I felt as if it were calling my name. "Could we have this room?" I asked. He told me he would have to go downstairs and ask his wife, since she set up all of the reservations. When he came back upstairs, he told us the room was taken the next night and since we were staying for two nights he couldn't let us have it. My heart sank. It had all seemed so perfect. Anyone who knew me and had seen this room would agree. I turned to Preston in disappointment, and we were taken to a room called "The Galaxy" suite. As I entered, I could feel the energy was quite different, and it made me feel rather uncomfortable. Not an angel in sight in this room. It just wasn't me. As I unpacked, I became more and more uncomfortable. At that point, however, I didn't have much of a choice. All of the other rooms were taken. I knew there was a reason I was in this room, but, between my ego and spirit, there was a struggle. I decided to wait, knowing that the angels would bring me the answer.

We headed out into the town now, and, as I walked out onto the front porch, the peaceful scenery took away my feeling of disappointment. I had asked the angels for a sign, and I knew they would bring it to me when the time was right. We walked towards the green and right away I connected with two women who were also visiting. One was from Indiana and the other from Ohio. They were training to become mediums and had just come from a class. We spoke easily as if we had known each other for years. They were as delighted as I was to be in this peaceful, spirit filled town. We chatted, and then they told us there was a service about to take place at the church. In the spiritualist religion, there is a protocol as in most churches. The minister stands at the podium and greets everyone. Songs are then sung to "raise" the vibration, and then a guest speaker comes forth to talk about "life" and spirit.

After the talk, a local medium who is part of the church stands and brings messages from loved ones who have passed. I found the whole service to be loving, cleansing and enlightening. The first day we were there the talk was on "aliveness" and how we are truly spirit having a human experience. It was funny because just before going to Lily Dale I had met a woman from California who did a talk on that very subject. Remember, there are no coincidences. She also spoke about spirits that are "stuck" here on the earth plane, and how we can send them towards the light. I had come across this several times in my readings and always found it to be quite fascinating. Now the minister was speaking about the difference between ego and spirit, and how we are truly spirit-filled if we choose to call upon this energy in our lives. As she spoke, I could feel her commitment to mankind, and a sense of divine peace that was being nourished by the choices she had made. She spoke for about 20 minutes, and by then the energy in the room was very high. A sixth generation spiritualist now proceeded to channel loved ones who had passed. She would point to certain people in the church and the words would flow quickly and with ease. She seemed to be right on target. Loved ones who sat in the pews were comforted, as a confirmation of their loved ones' energy was present in the room. As I left the service the first day, I had formed a "kinship" with those around me. It was effortless and came very naturally. I then thought to myself "what if it was like this in all the cities and towns around the world?" Just stop for a moment and imagine the connection we could all make at this level of spirit. It was almost too large to fathom, and so I felt I had stumbled upon a gift, a gift that would remain with me for many years to come.

As we left the church, we headed over to another very spirit filled spot in the woods known as "inspiration stump." Down the path we walked, towards the opening which housed benches on three sides, and the special "stump" at the head. Preston and I were the first to arrive, and as we walked along the path the woods surrounded us, and the sun shone through with a brilliant light that seemed to dance through the trees. As I walked along, I could feel energy all around me. Spirit was everywhere, and it felt as if loved ones were lining up to come through with their messages. I remarked to Preston that we were not alone. He agreed, and we continued to walk towards the stump. We sat in the front row that afternoon, and shortly after that the seats began to fill.

People from all over the country and the world were there waiting to hear messages from departed loved ones. The mediums were called up one by one to bring their messages. As we sat off to one side, the first medium to come up was a slender red- headed woman. She looked all around and then directly at me. "May I come to you?" is what she said. I said "yes" and she proceeded to talk about several loved ones of mine who had passed. First, she mentioned a woman, a grandmotherly type who was like a mother to me growing up. She told me that she was small with a good size chest and beautiful hazel eyes. I knew it was my grandmother right away, and she proceeded to tell me that she was around me guiding and supporting me. She also mentioned my father, and described him to a T. She said that my father and I had formed a partnership, and that our work together would continue to grow. She also said that I was doing a lot of healing work, and that my channeling was truly a gift. She told me I would help many, and how proud my father was of me. It was funny because she said I was about to help a woman who was in a lot of pain, and through my work I would help her to heal. I wrote it all down before she went on to the next person. She also told me that in the fall my healing capabilities would heighten and many would come for help. She was very excited for me and told me that spirit was working with me daily, and that all I had to do was "listen." I thanked her, and she proceeded to talk to others in the group.

At the end, we left and I had a true confirmation of the path I was following. Spirit was truly there for me, and as they guided and supported me I would agree to be a channel for their work.

As we headed back through the wooded path I felt that I had come to the right place. I loved the peaceful and serene energy that emanated from the woods, and as I re-entered the town I felt as if I was "at home" and peaceful within myself. As we walked along the streets, I saw a shop that had some of Lily Dale's finest treasures. I bought several items for gifts and something for myself. It was a beautiful shop filled with spirit and light. No pressure, just a commitment to helping those who entered. It was just around dusk when we entered the healing service in the chapel. The healers were lined up in the front, and people would go and sit down in front of them for healing. I waited and when the time was right I sat in front of a woman who placed her hands on my shoulders. We didn't talk, but I could feel the heat emanating from her hands. She worked on different parts of my body and then blessed me. I felt peaceful and serene as I went back to my seat. The energy in the chapel was both loving and healing. Preston also sat with one of the healers, and that night we both felt as if a transformation had taken place. As we went out into the night air, a warm breeze was coming from the lake. We headed down towards the town green and ate at the cafeteria in the center of town. The food was healthy and delicious. It was dark as we left the cafeteria, and the night was clear and the sky full of stars. It was very peaceful, and so we took our time going back to the inn.

On our way back we came across two women whom we had seen in the church. It was a woman and her daughter from Ontario who had come to Lily Dale for the first time. It was funny because the woman was my age, and her daughter was just about the same age as Cristina. We talked about the service and the stump, and her daughter said it was all a little overwhelming. She didn't quite know how she felt about it all. She was a little frightened and yet intrigued about the happenings in the quaint New York town. She told me she wasn't used to "knowing" that loved ones and spirit were around, and it kind of "spooked" her out. I told her of my work with the angels, and she asked me if I spoke to "dead" people. I told her I connected with those on the "other side" and didn't look at them as dead, but rather that they were on another "level." She found it to be quite interesting. Her mother told us that she had brought her daughter to Lily Dale to get more in touch with her own spirit. We shared our stories and ideas, and then headed back to our room. Little did I know that I myself would come across a spirit that very night!

We got ready for bed, and as I turned out the light, I had a sense that Preston and I were not alone. This never really bothered me because I felt this every night in my own bedroom. Spirits would come in to check on me and sometimes bring me messages or healing. I drifted off to sleep when suddenly I was awakened by the voice of a woman. She said her name was "Amanda," and that she needed my help. She had been stuck on the earth plane in this very room for a long time, and she was very tortured and depressed. At first, I didn't quite know what to do, and then as if a bolt of lightening hit me, I remembered the service that afternoon at the church. At that point, I asked her if she was willing to accept my help, and she said "yes." I started to send her white light, and told her she had nothing to fear. I told her to go towards the light now, and she would be free. She was very apprehensive, and we went back and forth for quite some time. It felt as if she was afraid because of something that had happened when she was alive. The room we were in was her room, and she had been trapped in spirit waiting for a release. All I could feel is that something had happened to her and she was ashamed. I didn't ask any more questions, and I continued talking to her in a soothing and loving way. I told her that the angels would take her up and she had nothing to fear. She started to sob and told me she had been abused after her mother passed away, and she felt destined to relive the situation over and over again. I could feel her pain, and told her it was time to let it all go. She continued to sob, and, finally, at around 6:00 a.m., she told me she was ready to put her fear aside and go towards the light. Her energy seemed to just disappear, and at that point I knew that she had been released. It was as if a huge brick was lifted off of my chest, and at that point I fell into a deep sleep.

I woke up around 9:00 a.m. and told Preston what had happened. The energy in the room seemed lighter and easier. I had my answer. I had to stay in that particular room to help this woman and release her to the other side. The angels also came through loud and clear to let me know that it didn't matter where I slept for they are with me wherever I am. It also dawned on me that the medium at the stump had told me I would help a woman who was in a lot of pain, and that healing would take place. I believe she was right, and I believe Amanda was that woman. God Bless you Amanda, may you fly high in the heavens, and may peace surround you always!

At that point, we decided to stay for the day, then leave and head to Buffalo that night. We were going to spend several days at Niagara Falls. I had never seen the falls and was excited about doing this. We had booked an 8 hour tour for Friday on the Canadian side along with all the activities that went along with it.

The rest of our time in Lily Dale was relaxing and rejuvenating. We went to another meeting at the stump, and, this time, I had the pleasure of connecting with my deceased husband, Walter. One of the mediums came to me again and picked me out of the group. She told me that there was a man who had fathered a beautiful little girl. She told me he had dark curly hair and that he watched over both of us. She described my daughter at three years of age in a dress that I had made for her. She told me he was sorry he had to go but that he was with us always. I knew it was Walter because Cristina was three when he passed. I could feel him around me, and knew he would come through. All of my feelings had been confirmed.

We left the stump and moved on to the service at the church. It was Preston's birthday, and I had truly hoped his mom would come through. I had a feeling she would come at the stump, but she was the kind of woman who did things in her own time. We sat at the service singing the songs and listening to the speaker. As the medium came to the podium to begin her work, I had a strong sense that Preston's mom was in the room. We had sat off to the side and the medium pointed to Preston. "May I come to you, sir?" "Yes, you may." Preston had been a spiritualist for over ten years and knew the protocol well. "I see a woman, a motherly type who is telling me that she is with you." She mentions bottles and needles and wants to thank you for being with her until the end." Christine Campbell had died of cancer, and before her passing, she had endured many tests and had to drink bottles of stuff she really hated. She also had many shots for the pain. "She is now at peace and wants you to know she loves you very much." Tears came to my eyes and it was funny because she had a message for me, as well. She told me to write all of this down, that it was very important. Thanks, Christine, I am happy to know you are well and happy on the other side.

She had waited to come on his birthday to bring her dear son a message. Preston was very happy that she had come through, and that he decided to come to Lily Dale. The both of us had connected with loved ones, and were grateful for the peace and tranquility of the Lily Dale experience.

Before leaving the Dale, we ate lunch and walked along the lake. It was starting to cloud up, and the wind began to blow. We sat for a few minutes and decided it was time to leave. A feeling of regret started to come over me for I would miss the peace that this little spirit-filled town nestled in the woods of Upstate New York had provided. As we headed back to the town, I would come across one more person for whom spirit had a message. She was a young woman around 30, and she was coming out of one of the shops. A pure white cat crossed our path, and we both reached out to pat her. As I looked up, our eyes connected, and I asked her if she was a resident of Lily Dale. She said "no," that she was taking classes on spiritual development, and that she was confused. I told her of my work with the angels, and she got very excited. "I would like to connect with the angels myself but don't know how." I knew I had been put there at that very moment for a reason. The angels wanted to help, and guide this woman so that she could overcome her fears and insecurities. I told her how the angels had come to me, and that all she had to do is ask and listen. I told her that she had to trust what came through, and as she did the angels would bring more. It's really all about "trust" and "desire." When spirits know you are willing, they present themselves." "I never thought about it that way, "she said." "Thank you," you have truly helped me to change my perception of spirit. We hugged, and at that moment, Preston pulled up in the car and we drove back through the gates. It was funny because as we drove out I could feel the energy shifting.

Thank You, Lily Dale for being there, and for all the spirit that came through to confirm that as humans we are truly not alone.

Niagara Falls was absolutely beautiful. The spirit of the falls reminded me of all of the beauty that God has put here on this earth for us. Since we had left one day earlier from Lily Dale, we were able to book the tour on Thursday instead of Friday. It was the perfect day and the tour a total success. The angels had guided us all the way, and I know more than ever that, as spirits having a human experience, we are guided each and everyday. All we have to do is stop for a moment or two, and listen.

A Tribute To Lily Dale

You came to me, so clear so true
I felt a pull, I must see you
So Lily Dale is where I head
The peace, the love, I must be fed

For spirit dwells so strong so clear
In Lily Dale, there is no fear
The healing that takes place each day
The service full of love and play

The stump a place where spirit flows
Where faith in heaven begins to grow
The angel inn up on the hill
A place where spirit comes to fill

The emptiness that dwells within
Is filled with belief, we are all kin
For a brotherhood of spirit lay
In Lily Dale in each new day

So as I leave your gates so fine
I know I will return in time
For once you've felt the spirit call
It's Lily Dale above them all

I wave goodbye and shed a tear
My time was spent in love not fear
So thank you for your kind embrace
Oh, Lily Dale, in all your grace

A week has gone by, and Lily Dale is still fresh on my mind. Several times this week I have looked back on the many events that happened, and I look forward to the day when I will return. This morning, as I start my channeling session, the angel, Kaeylarae comes to bring us her love and guidance. She is the angel of peace, and her commitment to humanity is admirable.

Channeling Kaeylarae

Look at your life at this very moment. How fortunate you are to have what is by your side. It is time to put aside the shadows that often bring upset and disillusion to us all. Look beyond the maze and see what is true. There will be connections with others on many levels. Not just the people who are coming in, but the people who are leaving, as well. So much has been accomplished, and the learning great, but above it all, choosing "peace" is the key. Healing can take place in any situation if peace is the goal. Who is right? Who is wrong? There is only one answer to this each and every time peace, understanding, and acceptance. If we trust that we are closing one door and opening another, then all there is to do is take a deep breath, and allow peace to enter our spirit. The journey has just begun. Do not allow the old to damage the new. Who is right? Who is wrong? Once again, I say there is no such thing. Our friends and loved ones have done us a favor when they push us out of the nest. Thank them, and know that you have grown, and that you are ready to take the next step. Don't be afraid. Allow the joy of adventure to envelop you. Your journey is your school, and you haven't time to look back. Peace is yours if you choose to take it. I, Kaeylarae, invite you to walk with me, so that I might share my thoughts of peace with you. I hand you a lily which brings you the peace you so deserve. It also represents the peace and joy that are on the horizon. Embrace the new, bless the old, and move forward with the confidence that you are truly on the right path. A path that allows the energy of "peace" to fill your soul.

This morning, as I sit down to channel, I feel the energy of Raphael around me. Yesterday had been a challenging health day for me and my "female" troubles had come to a head. I know in my heart that Raphael was around me, and I realized that the purging I had gone through was necessary for healing. This morning, as I choose the card for the day, the word "release" is presented to me. I feel the word pertains to a release from a female problem that had been going on for about a month. This particular morning, Raphael comes through bringing us the gifts of clarity and healing. Here is what he had to say.

Green

Healing

&

Restoring
Harmony and
Balance

Channeling Raphael: Healing Is Eminent

I have heard your cry and have come to present the concept of healing. It is unlike me to talk a lot but in this case I am sure it will make a difference. First of all, I want you to know that all of humanity is under the misconception that healing is something that is outside of oneself. What is healing? Ask yourself this question now. As I look down upon the earth I see that it is different for every human. Some think of healing as ridding oneself of pain. Others think of it on a spiritual level. This will bring a shift in one's way of thinking. Is the doctor truly the vehicle for healing? Does the touch of the reiki master heal your wounds, or is it God himself who brings forth his special touch. All of these ways can bring us closer to a possible healing, but the true healer is within ourselves. Do you truly know what your body does for you each and everyday? Do you treat your body with love, kindness, and generosity? Or do you take it for granted and often abuse the beautiful host that carries your precious soul upon this earth? Do you truly know how your body works, and what it needs to nourish and replenish itself on a daily basis? Or are you oblivious to its needs as you count on outside forces to "heal" what you have hurt. Healing starts with you. Healing is but a concept that is used very loosely, and as I look upon the humans who call upon spirit for help, I ask that they first look inside. What is it that causes your pain and suffering? This is a lesson for you to learn. To cover up and run from the truth is not the answer, for this is not the way to heal. Healing is a choice. It is there for you every moment of every day, and can be called upon in a split second. Do not separate yourself from your body for you are one. I am here to help, but first I want you to look inside for the answers. Once you have done this, the two of us can work as a team to bring forth the healing that is so needed. Sit quietly now, and look deep inside. What is the pain trying to tell you? Ask and listen for the answers will come. Now ask yourself the question: What is it that I need to do, dear body, to nourish you, and heal the wounds that I have created? Again, listen for the answer, for it is there. It may come through at that very moment or during your daily travels. The key is to listen, and look forward to the answer, for it is always present, and so you will be healed.

The love of God is flowing through me now. I am revitalized and renewed.

Raphael's huge emerald green wings are always there to comfort and heal us. Try wrapping them around you when you need his love and support.

After channeling Raphael this morning, I felt compelled to share this process with you. I like to call it "The Body Appreciation Mediation." I have had great success using this in the morning as a jump-start to my day, or during the day when I feel like I need to acknowledge and energize my body.

Channeled From Angelic Guidance: Loving And Rejuvenating Our Bodies

First, make sure you are in a comfortable position with your eyes closed. No noise or phone to disturb you. Take several deep cleansing breaths and relax.

The next step is to scan your body from head to toe. Remember all the parts of your body that support you each and everyday. The words go as follows: I now send love, thanks, and the universal white light of healing to my entire body. With light flowing to each system, and with the words of gratitude, you will stop, and acknowledge each and every part of your body as you send this healing love and light throughout each and every cell. Start at the top of your head, and work down stopping briefly at each organ as you bless and send the universal healing light. Do this always with a smile on your face for this boosts the immune system as well.

After you have done each organ, send this wonderful healing energy to your bones, muscles, tendons, blood, lymphatic, skin, hair, nail, teeth. You get the idea. When you have covered every inch of your body you will stretch gently, and claim good health in this new day. Your energy will soar, and your body will truly feel appreciated and loved.

Now go about your day treating your body to an array of nourishing foods and beverages. Don't forget to feed your mind with positive uplifting thoughts. Just by making this choice you have made a huge leap towards perfect health and well being.

Healing Waves From The Angels

On a warm spring evening, as I drift off to sleep, I feel a presence and a love that seems to surround me from head to toe. As if a wave of brilliant white light comes towards me, I feel this healing and supportive energy. First, it starts at my head, and even with my eyes closed, I can feel these brilliant waves of light coming towards me one after the other. Then as if they have done their job, they start to flow towards my chest, and then down to my waist, hips, legs, and buttocks until they reach my feet. Once this has happened, I feel light and very ethereal. It's almost as if the angels are letting me know exactly how they feel in their form. As I drift off to sleep, the waves continue to flow up and down my body. I want to thank the angels for their love and healing energy, for they know that at this time I need all the tender loving care I can get. Remember that this energy is always available to you. All it takes is a desire to connect with your angels. They will do the rest.

The Angel Paschar Imparts His Words Of Wisdom

The excitement builds inside of me as I channel Paschar this afternoon. It has been a harrowing day for me, and the challenges have been many. I ask for the angels' help, and when I look down at my angel deck, Paschar has come forth to bring me comfort and hope.

Channeling Paschar

Your desire is my desire. I am here to show you that you and you alone can call forth the energies to heal, as well as to have what it is that you want in your life. It is so simple, and yet as humans, I can see that you feel it is like climbing a mountain. This is so far from the truth, for spirit is here to guide you, and help you discern what is real as it removes all of the illusions. Your intention creates your reality, and so what will you choose to create? I say that if your vision is clear that all obstacles will be removed, and then the skies will open up bringing your deepest desires to fruition. I ask that you take the time now to ask yourself the question. What is it that I truly want in this situation? Now, picture this coming to you, and so it is. It is time to put aside all doubt and fear, and to claim what is truly yours. Whether it is a situation with a loved one, your health and wellbeing, or a financial problem, your vision will take you to the place where you want to go. You must know that you are capable of this, and that you must "envision" it as if you already have it. To hold your intention without fear or doubt, and to know that all is possible. You are much stronger, and more capable than you may have ever imagined. I now invite you to use this power to create that which you feel has been lacking in your life. I am here to support and help you along the way. You are never alone, and the prize is closer than you think." Vision it first; have patience so it can manifest; then watch, as the universe helps you to bring forth your true intention and purpose, here on earth.

I Had A Vision

I woke up this morning, my vision is clear
I've learned what's important, and let go of fear
My energy soars, for I can now be
The vision I've hoped for, the vision I see

I am an example of the vision I hold
A vision so powerful, a vision so bold
The choice I have made it, for I have free will
The learning and growth, how they both fit the bill

Intention is strong, as strong as can be
I pull pure intention, now closer to me
The angels they guide me, so fresh and so bold
My spirit is soaring; I've now met my goal

Paschar, he reminds me, so upward I fly
I soar towards my dreams, joy filling my cry
The goodness it flows, my arms open wide
As free as a bird with no need to hide

Now I hold my desire so close to my heart
Paschar he surrounds me, and we are never apart
So I ask you right now "what vision do you hold?"
It's your turn to look and your life will unfold

No fear and no doubt for it blocks your success
Move onward and upward away from the mess
That often confuses our minds, and once clear
Hold tight to your vision, all doubts disappear

It's your special dream to create in your life
So I ask you to put away struggle and strife
Remember "intention" success it will bring
"Alleluia, alleluia," the angels will sing

Starting The Week Off Right

It is Monday morning, and as I sit and ask the angels to bring their love and guidance to all who open their hearts and minds, it occurs to me that I must mention "God's" intention. God brings forth his angels for us to befriend as they guide us along the way. There are many names for "God" and many different religions, but I have never heard or read about a religion that didn't make mention of some sort of angel. I know that the names may be different, but there is a spirit form of help from up above and the term "Angel" is just that. It never ceases to amaze me when I ask the angels for their love and guidance, for in some way, in that very moment, I know that they hear me, and that they are going to work to provide me with some sort of answer. Again, it may not happen in that very second, but as my day starts to unfold, and if I listen, and stay aware, then the answer will come. It doesn't always present itself in the way I thought it might, but it does show up. As I sit here this morning and ask for angelic guidance, the angel, Zacharael comes forth. Zacharael is connected with the number "seven" which is unions, and, in this case, surrendering to "God". Zacharael brings forth this message from God himself. He lets us know that God is present in our lives and always willing to support us. I have had several very powerful sessions when the presence of God was strong. The room became very still, and the energies that entered were loving and all-powerful. Here are the words that Zacharael brings to us today.

Channeling Zacharael Who Asks Us All To Surrender

Children of God, I come to you this morning with words of support and guidance. Stop as you read this and internalize all that it means. Put aside the fight. Surrender to what is out of your hands. It is time to look deeper, and to trust and have faith. All is not lost—it is only put aside for the moment. Calm yourself. Know that there is a power above all powers, and yet this power in itself is gentle and kind. You have the capability now to release all that is on your mind. Place all that burdens you into a cloud which can rise above and be dissolved. You are not alone and never have been. God comes with all of his wisdom now, and if you listen for the words that are spoken, you will feel his devotion and love. This is what will get you through. This is what will make you know that you are unique, and so very loved. That there is no one quite like you. In God's eyes you are so very special. Throw away the misconception, the old beliefs, and the fear of who you think you are, for you are part of God's great universe, and you will not be forsaken. So I ask you in this new day to become vulnerable to your heavenly father. Trust that this too shall pass, and the light of the heavens will shine upon you with the answers that you so yearn. Universal law will be upheld, and you will walk along your path hand in hand with God and his angels. Take his hand right now, and watch as you are guided into the perfect place. This is the time for you to make the choice. Doubts and fears will only stand in the way; release this through the breath, as you envision the peace that is waiting to enter your soul.

A Message From God

For you are my children and precious to me. I will not leave your side, but I encourage you to connect with the part of yourself that is God, for you have been given everything you need if only you will open your eyes and see what is right in front of you.

A Mini-Mediation To Help You Release And Move On

Take three deep cleansing breaths. You are relaxed at this time and you are aware of what it is you want to let go of. Now, with eyes closed, picture your situation. At this time, you will place it into a "Golden Basket." Make sure you have put every bit of the situation inside now, and call upon Zacharael who will take your problem up into the heavens for an answer from God. This situation is now in God's hands, and will be taken care of at the right time. Go about your day with confidence knowing that your problems are being addressed and taken care of. This is a true acknowledgement of faith, knowing that God will not let you down. When the time is right, the answers will come, and you will be able to make the right choice, a choice that is made with faith and free from fear.

A Message From Nisroc

Nisroc asks that you look at your life and see where you feel stuck. He is here to help you decide the direction you want to go, and to help you to see that often it is our minds, more than our situation, that keep us under the illusion that we are trapped.

Channeling Nisroc And The "Keys" To Freedom

You and you alone are feeling that you are imprisoned in your life situation. Earth is full of situations that create a sense of entrapment, and from this a great lesson is to be learned. What is it that makes you feel so compromised? What situation do you want to escape from in your life? I ask that you look deep within, and make sure that it is worth the effort. For what is the lesson that can be learned from this situation? Who or what is holding you back? Are you too connected, and need to step aside to see the "bigger" picture? Or are you just too stubborn to move forward? These are the questions you must ask yourself. You must see if these feelings run deeper than you thought. What is the real cause of your pain? Is it something that started a very long time ago, and this situation has reopened your wound? Or is it truly what is present at this time in your life? It is time for the truth to come forth. Healing will manifest out of honesty, and freedom will be the outcome. "I am free; I am clear; I am flowing in this new day." These are the words that will bring about the biggest change. When you are ready, you will find these words comforting and a source of healing. First, you must know the lesson, and, by doing this, freedom will come. I am with you and will guide you if you call upon me for help. I will help you to dispel the illusion. Clarity will be the outcome, and from this you will become "crystal clear." This lesson is but another key to your freedom. Be willing now to delve deep inside and put aside the need to be righteous, for another part of the healing is the willingness to be honest and loving with yourself.

A Tribute To Aunt Annette

Looking back on my childhood, I recall the large Italian family that contributed to my upbringing. I was one of the first born, and so from the beginning I was taken care of and watched over by my grandparents, aunts, and uncles. Each and every one of my mother's eight brothers and sisters played a significant role in my life. Many lessons were learned, challenges arose, yet a love and appreciation for each one of them prevails.

My eldest Aunt whose name was "Annette" passed away several years ago rather suddenly. She had been born in Italy and had come to America as a young child. Growing up she taught me patience, and how to be kind when I really wanted to lash out and put my aunt in her place. Her moods were rather erratic, and I often disagreed with some of the things she did, especially as I grew older. It was funny, but as I watched my aunt grow in age and shrink in size, I realized that life had not dealt her the easiest set of circumstances.

Lonely most of the time, Aunt Annette had plenty of money but the one thing that she yearned for was missing. She had been married several times but each marriage had been more of a subservient position rather than a love connection. It was sad to see her unhappiness, and I would often wish that she would find either a special someone to calm and soothe her tattered nerves, or that she would find a purpose to feed her aching soul. In the end, neither had happened, and as I sat by her bed she grew weaker, as her time on earth began to dwindle. I told her that I loved her and that she would soon be in God's hands. "The angels will guide you, don't be afraid." She didn't move. Her sleep was deep and part of me thought that she was already on the other side, although she was still breathing. When the time came, I felt a great sense of relief, knowing she was at peace. She had filled her karma here on earth, and would leave a large sum of money behind to loved ones, money that she had never really enjoyed or used. It was sad but true. Could this have been her purpose here on earth? To leave loved ones the money that she had saved for years. Quite a sacrifice in-deed! Part of the money would help put my daughter through college, and would also help other family members in need. She also donated a great amount to charity, which in itself was very admirable. As I sit here this morning, I think about Aunt Annette and her contribution to my life. Not just in monies, but in lessons, and I thank her for being so devoted to her family. I have a belief that the people who bring us the biggest challenges also teach us the greatest lessons. One of the items that I received from my dear Aunt's passing was an angel clock that chimes every hour. As it sits in my angel room, it will often times bong just as I am about to do a reading. I feel it is a sign that Aunt Annette is there watching over and helping the energy to flow. It will often chime when it shouldn't, and I truly know she is bringing forth spirit energy from above. This is for you, Aunt Annette. I hope that your journey has been joyous, and that you sit with God and his angels in the Kingdom of Heaven.

Lessons Of Love

Upon the ship that sailed from Rome
So far away from her native home
You venture out, lands far away
Your life will change in this new day

For promise of a better life
One full of joy instead of strife
So as you enter the land of the free
So many faces you will see

For all are seeking the freedom here
The test begins; it's crystal clear
A child has hopes and dreams inside
She hopes that happiness will reside
Among the streets that pass her by
So different here in many ways
She wonders, "Will there be time for play?"

A tug now comes from deep inside
America's here with all its pride
And as she grows in this new land
She waits for the promise for "which it stands"

The years fly by; the sadness grows
For life has dealt Annette the blows
But as she enters the gates above
It's home, it's home, she feels the love

From God and all the spirit there
Her hopes and dreams without despair
This is the place where the joy resides
She's finally home where spirit lies

Aunt Annette's Wisdom

The angel Gabriel has come through this morning with the promise of resurrection for all of us here on earth. It seems so appropriate, and once again I feel like Aunt Annette has requested that Gabriel come through. The promise of "New Life," whether it is a fresh start here on the earth plane, or the promise of "Life after Death," Archangel Gabriel has much to say.

Channeling Gabriel

It is time for all of mankind to look at life as a precious gift, for often times this is forgotten. Now is the time to make the change; now is the time to wake up and see what you are doing. The time is "ripe" and you are ready to walk through all of the illusion, for on the other side you will find the new beginning that is waiting for you. This does not mean you are leaving the earth plane, but in essence you are leaving all of the old baggage behind. A fresh energy has emerged, and you are part of this. Do not despair, for much help is on its way. The guidance that accompanies these changes is strong, and you will know which way to go if you stop and listen. Your "gut" feeling will guide you onto the right path, and it is from there that you will create the new life that is waiting for you. Shed the old skin now and watch as you become lighter, and life becomes a joy once more. Take the lessons, and cherish them for they are truly a gift from above; move into the place where fresh air resides. Do not look back; move forward with joy and ease. The time has finally come for your path to take a turn. Rejoice in all the blessings that it brings, knowing that God and his angels watch over you and guide you as your journey begins.

New Life

The time has come, it's crystal clear
Move onward and upward, no doubt, no fear

For life is following a different path
A pull that feels so right, so sure
A pull that asks us to endure

For at the end the light will shine
So focus now and don't decline
For the doors they are about to open
The words they flow, some are unspoken

For spirit guides us on our way
Its faith and trust so don't delay
Allow the fresh and vital flow
Shed all the old, and you will grow

So it's on to a bigger and better life
One full of joy, no longer strife
I ask you now to just let go
Let spirit take you with the flow

You're almost there so don't give up
It's time, it's time to fill the cup
You have arrived, this too is clear
Let spirit guide, no doubt, no fear

Full circle you have come this day
Enjoy, enjoy, new life—hooray!

The Glorious Truth

As the sun shines bright this morning in Hanover, Massachusetts, I sit and ask for guidance. The angel, Amitiel, comes to bring us the importance of "truth." We have all heard terms like "The truth will set you free," and "Honesty is the best policy." Spirit comes to ask us the questions: "What is your truth?" "How will you use this truth as you go about your day?"

Most of us find it hard to be honest at times. Being totally honest can be frightening. Often we fear that we will hurt someone we love, or that we might lose something that we're not ready to let go of.

The following is a channeling session with Amitiel who brings us an angelic perspective on the "Truth."

Channeling Amitiel Who Ushers In The Truth

No longer can you look at what is false. Honesty flows from your lips, and what is true will be present. It is not so easy, but one must know that help is always available. Your truth may not be the same as your friends! So many different versions of the truth appear, and so you must look deep inside for your own personal truth. Once you have discovered this truth, you will live by it, and so you will attract others with similar truths. It is hard to see at first but as you relax, and take on this responsibility, it will become easier and easier. Is your friend truly a friend or a reflection of your own dishonesty? A hard question to ask yourself, but by answering this question you will become free from the lies that have surrounded your life. Know what your integrity is and put aside the fears that come to the surface. Yes, it is true—"The truth will set you free." Do not hold onto the anger. Release this in a safe and nurturing way. Why should you carry this around with you when the truth is available in this very moment? Courage is part of this truth, and by being "true" to yourself you will find the courage to pursue that which is your personal truth in all situations. Being responsible for your life in all situations is a good place to start. Once you know that you play a role in this scenario, the outcome will be positive. Be honest, and loving with yourself, and see your vulnerabilities as an opportunity. Learning and growing together, you will see that others are seeking the truth as well. Be a patient and loving example for others for that is truly your spirit at work. Call upon me often for guidance, for I promise to help you see the truth in all situations.

Telling The Truth

This technique is one that I've adopted through my ventures. I find it to be cleansing and helpful when you feel an injustice has been done to you. It is a way to release the anger in a "safe" space and will enable you to see the "true" picture so you can move forward.

Some call this the **"Truth Process;"** others call it the **"Love Letter."**

I feel it is all part of forgiveness and release.

Say that a friend, loved one, co-worker or just about anyone that you deal with in your life has upset you in some way. You can't seem to let it go and you start to dwell on it, and it becomes a nagging problem. I find that when I use the process below it helps me to release the anger, as well as to start the forgiveness process that is so important. The following is a list of steps to start and complete this process. You will be writing a letter to the person, so get plenty of paper and a good pen to start.

Make sure you have enough time to complete the process; this all depends on what you have to say.

Remember this is the "Truth Process" so you must say what is on your mind. Remember not to judge yourself; just be honest. Everything that you would want to say if you could is what goes on the paper; just write it out in any way that feels good. I would call this an "Ego" purging of sorts.

When the emotions start to surface, there may be some rather nasty thoughts that come to mind. Just write them down. This is how we get to the core of our feelings. Again, no guilt and no holding back. There will be many feelings that come up as you write this letter. First and foremost, there will probably be anger, then sadness, some fear and, last but not least, love and forgiveness.

As the anger is released, it may go on for some time. Know that this is fine, and that soon the sadness will come up around being hurt, and then the deep connection you have with this person will become very evident. You have been hurt and thought this person cared about you. It is time to let them know this, as you pour your heart out on the paper. This is a time of release, so please say whatever it is that you need say. Remember these trapped feelings are only getting in the way of forgiveness. Also, remember that forgiving someone doesn't mean that you are wrong and they are right; it is just a way to release the emotion around the anger and hurt which in turn brings clarity to the situation. Forgiving someone doesn't mean you have to "befriend" them either. Sometimes it just means that you wish them well but no longer choose to have them in your life. The choice is up to you. Remember that each soul that we meet has a special lesson to teach us. If we look beyond our emotions, often the lesson will present itself. This, of course, is a gift, and certainly a way to heal our relationships.

Now the anger is passing, and you start to share the hurt that you felt and how you really don't want this to get in the way of your relationship. You end by telling the person what they mean to you, and how you have found a space in your heart to forgive them. This, of course, only comes after you have purged all of your feelings. This may also bring up old hurts from the past which you can also address at this time.

I find that when I have ended this process I feel lighter, and happier and more open to healing the relationship. Give this a try and see how it works for you. Remember the key is to be open, and honest, and to purge everything you are feeling....no holding back. At the end you can tear the letter up or burn it. Stop for a moment; now take a deep breath, and feel the freedom.

This may also be a time to use the "Forgiveness and Release Process" for a few days to clear any remaining resentment. I promise you that you will not only feel ten pounds lighter, but others may ask you if you lost weight. Your eyes will shine once more, and you will have tons of energy. I find that this often "softens" the situation, and the person you were angry with will most likely approach you in some way. A greeting card may come in the mail with a loving message, or you may receive a phone call out of the blue.

Whatever happens just know that you have the "tools" to free yourself from the resentments that have been pulling you down. Remember that forgiveness is truly an awakening, and that if we look at all the people in our lives as "teachers," and we are open to learning the lessons, then forgiveness becomes easy and effortless.

There is no right or wrong just opportunities for love and transformation.

White

Purity

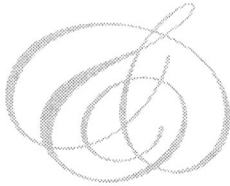

Expanding the Light

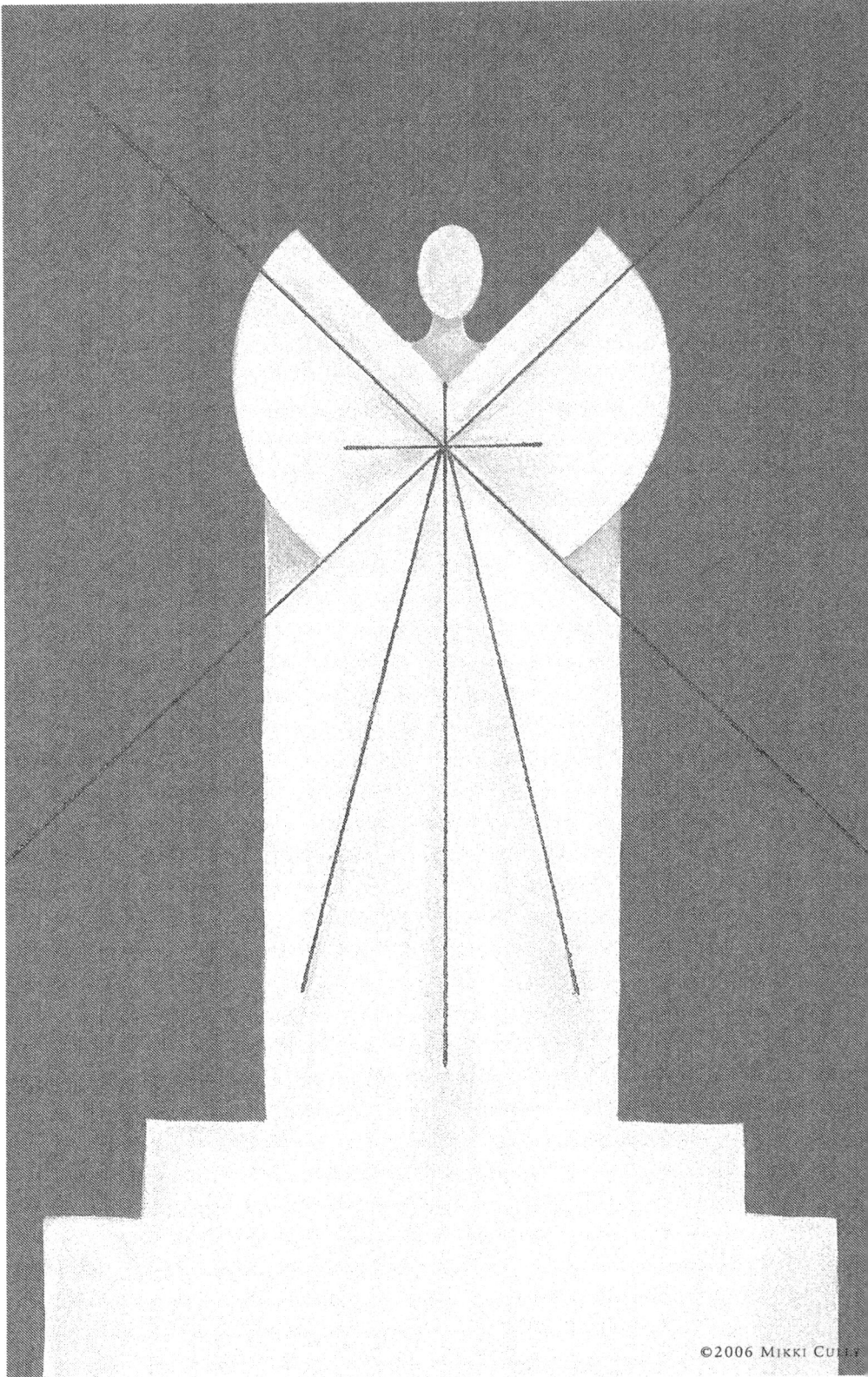

WHEN LIFE THROWS US A CURVE

There is no doubt in my mind that life is unpredictable. One recent example of this was the category 5 hurricane that hit the Gulf Coast on Monday the 29th of August, 2005. I was stunned to see the devastation, and as I watched this on my television for almost a week, I asked the questions that so many of you probably asked. Why is this happening and what will come of all the homeless men, women, and children of hurricane Katrina's fury?

Katrina,

As I watch the news this week, hurricane Katrina has hit the coast of Louisiana, Mississippi, and Alabama. As the wind and rain battered these areas, all I could think of is the word "cleanse" as I was reminded that the name Katrina means "to purify" and so it is. As I sit and watch the pain that the residents of these communities experience, I am reminded of our "times," so many events, so much taking place. The earth is changing; there is no doubt of that. It is hard to see such an event because it reminds us of the possibilities. One day we are here living out our lives in our homes that are warm and comfortable with plenty of food and water, and the next day we are out in the street with no place to go. It is a powerful yet painful learning experience. A sense of survival kicks in, and we reach out to help those in need. Others become full of fear and lash out committing violent acts to survive. It is certainly a mix of love and fear, emotions that we all experience every day. It has been six days since the storm hit, and my feelings have gone from appreciation of what I have in my life to sadness and compassion for those in need. All of the small children, the elderly, and people of all walks of life all in the middle of crisis. As I ask the angels for guidance, I am concerned for those who are still without food, and water, and for the people who no longer have a job or a place to live. Money is my first thought and I pool monies with

Preston and my mom to send to the needy. Somehow money still doesn't seem to be the answer. I send my love and prayers and healing, and pray for strength for the many who suffer. I remind myself that this is the "Earth Plane" and of course "School." I also try to remember that our souls are all-knowing, and that each experience we go through is for a reason and a purpose. Yet my heart goes out as I see the conditions that my fellow man must endure. We are all connected, and somehow although I have a warm cozy home, and plenty of food and drink, I am going through this, as well. I know that the angels are with them, and many miracles will come and already have. I ask the angels now what will be the outcome for the people and their homes, and at that moment it all became crystal clear. The angel Gabriel has come through as he brings the vibration of the "Resurrection" and "New Life." How appropriate, for out of this disaster, out of the chaos will come a clarity for all to behold.

Questions are always answered in time, and so on the sixth day I was given this information from "Gabriel, the angel of Resurrection."

Channeling Gabriel And New Life

The cleansing has begun. In time you will know that the purpose is for all to grow and move forward. There are no coincidences, and in this case, it is faith and trust that move you in the direction you need to go. Know that you are not alone. You are in the hands of God and his angels at all times. It is how it was meant to be, and you will come full circle through the devastation of these times. Forget not who you are, for you will discover a part of yourself that you didn't even know was there. Spirit is calling for your life to become fresh & new. It is the same for those who have made the journey to the other side, for they will be resurrected in God's Kingdom. It is now that your soul will venture out and display strength for all to see. Let go of the old now for the possessions are just that, and it is your inner desire to move forward that will carry you to a life that you so deserve. Allow spirit to guide you, and listen, for there is much to hear. As you purge the old, start to welcome the new. Now is the time to make the choice. Now is the time to know that you are capable of great things, for the resurrection is available to all who leave open the door to change.

It has been weeks since Katrina's fury battered the Gulf Coast. The commitment of our fellow human beings is truly admirable, and as I sit and watch the many who have donated their time, love, light and money, I am proud and moved to see the human spirit at work.

Angel In The Clouds

Over the years I have heard many stories that pertain to angels. One in particular was brought to my attention on September 1, 2005. Heather, who is a very good client of mine, told me about her friend, Amy, who had taken a rather incredible picture of an angel sitting above a rainbow among the clouds. I was very excited, and wanted to meet Amy, as well as to hear the story and see the picture she had taken. As both Heather and Amy entered my house, I felt privileged to receive this spirit-filled information. I served tea and muffins on the back porch and waited patiently to hear the story that Amy would share. She spoke of a friend who had passed away at the age of 60, and how he had wanted his ashes spread over the waters of Rockport, Massachusetts. His name was Ernie, and his life had been cut short by cancer. Amy explained how he had hung on for quite some time but in the end he had finally passed on, making the journey to the other side. She spoke fondly of him, and started to tell me just what had happened that day. Four boats left the docks sailing out into the bay to spread his ashes along the cool waters of the North Shore. A circle was formed, and since Ernie had a great fondness for Hawaii, everyone wore a lay around their neck. The ashes were spread, and the lays thrown into the water. The day was sunny and bright, and fair weather clouds floated gracefully in the blue sky above. As they positioned their boats and began the ceremony, the ashes were evenly sprinkled into the deep blue ocean. The prayers were said as the lays were cast. The mission was now complete. As the boats were just about to head back to shore, Amy and her brother happened to look up towards the sky and, lo and behold, a beautiful rainbow had appeared. As they looked closely, they could see a figure just above the rainbow. Looking even closer, they saw what appeared to be a pair of wings and a halo. Amy was in awe, as she saw the angel that was hovering above the rainbow. It was right over the area where the boats had sprinkled Ernie's ashes. A deep feeling of peace came over them, and they knew that Ernie was in the arms of the angels and home at last.

As Amy showed me the picture, there was no doubt in my mind; it was the outline of an angel sitting above the rainbow. She was there to let everyone who had participated in Ernie's farewell ceremony know that he was being guided and protected by spirit. What a comfort for all who knew and cared about their friend. As I sat and looked at the picture, I could feel Ernie's energy and his appreciation for life. I felt his kindness, and his devotion, as well as his humor, and love for all of those who had come to bid him farewell. I didn't know Ernie in this life, but somehow today I had caught a glimpse of his spirit. I felt compelled to write this poem, and feel that Ernie himself had a special message to leave all of those who cared so very much about him. This is just another example of the many "gifts" that the angels bring to us on a daily basis. This is for you, Ernie. May you live in the peace and love of the angels, our friends on earth and in heaven.

Ernie's Angel

There is a man named Ernie
Whom I just met today
His laughter and his humor
He brings along to say

That he resides in heaven
With angels on both sides
They took him up to heaven
A very special ride

His new home is so special
A place that's filled with light
No pain, no fear, no sadness
No need to win the fight

Now Ernie himself steps in:

For perfect is this place I live
The angels guiding me
So perfect in so many ways
It's God Kingdom that I see

So do not cry, my family
For I will wait for you
The gates they will be open
The angels will appear

They'll bring you up to greet me
A reunion oh so dear
So think of me from time to time
And I will think of you
Know angels are around us
In each and every day
They guide us and they help us
In work, at home, in play

And someday when they show up
To bring you for the ride
I'll see you in the heavens
Where we will all reside

A Special Day

Monday mornings seem to appear very quickly as we end our work week on Friday. This Monday happens to be Labor Day, 2005 and, as I sit here this morning, I must say that the weather is cooperating nicely, and the many trees in my backyard blending in with the deep blue sky brings joy to my heart. My channeling session this morning feels perfect. Just the kind of weather I love. Crisp, cool, sunny and delightful, September is upon us and the fall is starting to show us its tone. This is my favorite time of year. Soon the leaves will turn their many brilliant colors, and we will be headed north to see them in all their glory. Like the many people and creatures that inhabit the earth, the leaves display their uniqueness for all to see.

Zagzagel comes through this morning with her wisdom and love. She is adorned in a multitude of colors and so appropriate for this time of year. Oranges and browns with hints of gold and green. She brings us her guidance and speaks of wisdom and the power that it affords in our everyday lives.

I want to thank you Zagzagel for bringing us your words of wisdom.

Zagzagel's Speaks

Where are you going? And how do you plan on getting there? Your goals are set, and you feel confident that this is your path. It is time to look beyond the confusion once more and see the purpose of this choice. What is it that you want to create from this decision, and how will this affect those around you? Every day we must ask ourselves these questions. What gifts do you want to bring into your home on earth today? How will you display your unique self to others while showing and teaching them their own divine nature? Many pieces like a puzzle are part of the equation. Commitment, love, play, joy, and freedom are all parts of this collage. Waking up each morning and claiming the tone for that day are of the utmost importance. This is not about control, but about using spirit for guidance for the highest good of all concerned. Choices are made every minute, and you have the choice to come from the wisdom that lies deep within your soul. Remember that you are the vehicle for change, a change that not only affects you, but all who inhabit your space. Shine your light in this new day. Know your perfection as you share this with all who come your way. You will know what to do, and the energies will support you on your journey. Put aside the "ego" and come from the true essence of your being. I will be there to guide you. "Ask and ye shall receive." "Seek and ye shall find." Simple yet important scripture that tells all. Keep it simple now, and know that your divine nature will grow as you allow it to be present in your daily life. Once again, this is always a choice. Listen and you will hear the guidance that is coming your way. Enjoy your day, as you spread this joy to others, for they in turn will pass it on and so it goes. Like a beacon of light that shines for miles, your true essence and love will provide the guidance for others on their path. For truly there is no separation; we are all one.

Using Zagzagel's Wisdom

I myself will take Zagzagel's wisdom into my day and apply it to whomever I come in contact with. As I grow and learn about myself, I am given the lessons that I must learn. It is fascinating because the more I venture out and live in the question, the more "challenges" are presented to me. Awareness of course plays a big role in this, and I feel blessed to be aware of the happenings around me. As I look back on my life, I often feel that I have lived many lifetimes in this life. At age 51, I am looking back at lessons that started many years ago, and at the fact that I am finally starting to "get" their meanings. This is not a judgment but an observation. I know I have a choice in how I look at the happenings around me, and that I must look at how I play a role in them. Stepping away from being the "victim" is hard for most people, but I have found that when I take responsibility for what has been created a sense of "personal power" returns. My light becomes bright, and I have learned the lesson that has been presented. Over the years I have grown at times in leaps and bounds. I have seen others around me blossom, as well, and it always brings me great joy to see their lives unfold. Letting go is a big part of this lesson for me, and I am starting to practice this more and more. People come and go in our lives daily. Some stay for long periods of time, while others seem to be gone in the blink of an eye. Everyone who crosses our path has an important message to share. Whether it is the guy who cuts us off in traffic, or the good friend who shares his or her deepest secrets, it is in each new moment that we have the choice to come from our true selves. Bless those who stay as well as those who leave. Try not to take it personally remembering what you have learned from being with them. As they feel your blessing, they too will return this to you, and you will once again be on your journey of discovery. New faces will step in, and new experiences will present themselves. Staying attached will only bring pain, so let go. We may not always do this, and I myself know that I am human and sometimes allow my emotions to take control. Once again, this is earth, and earth is school, and we are all learning and growing at different rates. Give yourself a break. Know that you are progressing nicely, and pat yourself on the back often, for those of us who choose to inhabit the earth plane in these changing times should be commended. You are the healers, and the souls that will turn our planet around. If you are reading this, you know who you are. Remember to shine your light often and love yourself unconditionally, as God and his angels do. Perception is "key" and the choices you make decide the outcome. I like to define this power as a gentle yet all-enduring energy that only sees love. As you will see from the story below, intuition is very important, and timing truly does come from the "Divine."

Divine Timing

It is several days before my knee surgery, and twice the angels have come to say *"the time isn't right."* The first time I became very ill the night before, and no matter how much I prayed, or asked for help, the angels just weren't willing to budge. I could feel Remliel, the angel of mercy, once again warning me that something would happen that would not be for my highest good. It's funny because I had been waiting since November of 2004 to find out just what was wrong with my knee, and then received three different diagnoses until finally I talked my doctor into an MRI. There it was two torn pieces of cartilage which were causing much pain, swelling and discomfort. I had been on crutches for sometime, and recently switched to a cane. One thing for sure, the angels were guiding me all the way. The date was set—June 10th, 2005, but here I was the night before feverish and feeling very weak. Was it fear? Could I be causing this illness? As I lay there in bed, it became crystal clear that there was a force bigger than myself at work. Faith and trust had to be part of the equation, and so as I lay there praying that night I realized that it was all out of my control, and that I had to listen, and trust the information that was coming through. It was funny because several days later I heard that they had had a tuberculosis scare among the employees of the hospital. Huh, I thought. Was this the reason? But then as time went on, I was to meet one special lady who would shed light on what had happened. A dear friend and client by the name of Laura called me several weeks after I was to have surgery. We hadn't seen each other in quite some time, and I was delighted to hear from her. As we began to talk, she mentioned that she had had something quite unusual happen. She mentioned my surgery, and said that she had gone to a friend's house for a psychic reading the night before, and that the woman mentioned a friend named "Cathi." She told me that the woman told her that my surgery had been delayed, and that it was a good thing I didn't have it done. She mentioned that the "time" just wasn't right and the healing would not have been to my liking. Ah, I thought, the answers are starting to come. After my initial excitement, I decided to call and make an appointment. It was strange because as she answered the phone she told me that she was just stepping out the door but something told her to answer. As I drove up in front of her house, I felt a deep connection with my loved ones on the other side, and as I walked up the stairs she was waiting for me at the front door.   Her name was Barbara Jane, and she told me she felt a small man wearing a black hat entering the house with me.   She told me his name began with an S, and that he was my grandfather. It sure did sound like grampy. She told me he was guiding me, and that he was watching over me day and night.   As we traded services, I could see that many of my loved ones on the other side were supporting and working with me. As I asked her once again about the surgery, she told me that my loved ones were telling her that September would be the perfect time. I had already been given a date in July 19th, but didn't feel comfortable with that either.   Mercury would be retrograde, and I felt the energy would not be that supportive. I feel now that I made the right decision. Several other confirmations have come since then, and I feel confident that when I have the surgery on September 9th that all will go well. The number 9 stands for endings, and in this case I was ready. I also have a great belief in affirmation so I wrote a "perfect" scenario to accompany the love and guidance of the angels. There are no coincidences in life. When we come upon a situation that is "held up" or "pushed forward," we must trust that there is a reason. As I sit here this afternoon, I am visited by Cerviel, the angel of Courage. She is ushered in with the number eight which brings about the vibration of change and transformation. These are her words:

Channeling Cerviel Who Brings Courage To All

The angels come in groves to oversee this event. You are in special hands, my child, and we will guide the surgeon's hands as if they were our own. You are cherished and loved, and many pray for you at this time. The room is filled with light, and healing is imminent. Do not allow fear to keep you awake. Close your eyes now, and trust that all is being done for your highest good. Healing is the outcome and a return to wholeness. Our love for you is rich and deep. Surrender your doubts and fears. Float back into our arms, and allow us to surround you with light and protection. Loved ones stand by, and your true friends are those who wish you well, and send the light your way. Deep is our commitment to your healing. Raphael, the Virgin Mother, loved ones on the other side, and your angelic friends in heaven are with you at every moment. Jesus sits by your side. Glory is yours, for you have trusted God and his angels. This is a time of great accomplishment. We look forward to working with the healing energies that are all around. Bless the doctors so they allow their hands to be guided by the light. Let go now, and drift into a soothing sleep. Wake and feel refreshed and new again. The energies will flow, and healing will be the outcome.

Surgery—September 9th 2005

On the day before my surgery I am calm and relaxed. Much different from the first time when no matter what I did I was unable to calm my nerves and my upset stomach. The channeling from Cerviel has brought me much comfort, and I have full faith that all will go as planned. I have brought my "Healing with the Angels" tape along with my CD player hoping they will let me listen to it during the surgery. The morning is bright and warm, and we head into Boston with ease. Interesting because this was what I had affirmed for myself. As we enter the hospital, I am feeling rather positive, and we are greeted with kindness, as I am taken care of in a timely manner. Preston will wait for me in recovery, and he promises to send light during the surgery. I feel as if all my loved ones and concerned friends are with me. I feel their prayers and the angels' presence. My teacher, and good friend, Jaqui reminds me to hold Jesus' hand. "Allow him to sit with you during the surgery as I have many times in the past." Archangel Michael is in the room as is Raphael with his huge emerald green wings. I feel his love and healing energy all around me. The doctor comes in now and explains what he is about to do. I ask if I could have the nerve block, and twilight sleep, and he agrees. He also allows me to listen to my angel tape, and so off I go, confident that all will go well. As I drift off, I feel a very loving presence by my side and know my dear father, Americo Michael, is with me. As if in the blink of an eye, I am awake, and traveling down the corridor to recovery. Preston is there waiting for me, and the doctor tells us that it all went well. As I dress to go home, I am grateful that the surgery is over. The following is the affirmation that I had created about a month before my surgery.

This Is What I Choose To Create

Remember that we are all "creative beings," so what we choose to claim we can create.

I have scheduled my surgery on my left knee for the 9th of September. The day is sunny and bright, and I am feeling very positive about the outcome. I travel in with Preston easily and effortlessly, as the angels, spirit, and Jesus travel by my side. I have the very best surgeon, whom I trust, knowing he will do a wonderful job on my knee. My knee will heal quickly, and it will be better than ever. The day of my surgery everyone who is part of the surgical team will be alert and very willing to make sure that I am kept healthy, and that the surgery is a total success. I will wake up in the recovery room quickly, and feel very good about the outcome. The anesthesiologist is also the best, and does an excellent job making sure I get the nerve block and the twilight medicine in just the right dosage. I feel great going in because I know I will be well taken care of, and my surgery will be fast and successful. Thanks to all of the wonderful medical people who helped me to walk normally again. I bless you all, and send you love, light, and thanks.

Post Surgery

It has been several days since the surgery, and I am recovering nicely.

There is some pain, but I know that with a positive attitude and the help of spirit I will recover and once again return to the activities I enjoy. Over the years, I have had a great belief that we are creative beings who do have a choice regarding the events in our lives. Affirming and "claiming" what we want to bring towards us is a great part of this. The other part, of course, is our willingness to have the "right attitude". I, myself, have had many challenges in my life, and as I grow, I know that the one thing that I do have control over is my attitude. As each new day appears, I will create healing for myself with the help of my guides, the angels, and loved ones who wish me well. Try doing this affirmative process the next time you have to go though surgery or any life-changing event.

Partnership

As I continue to work with angelic energy this morning, I am reminded that as humans we are also partners on the earth plane. With different levels of partnership we are reminded of the many different connections that bring us together. In a traditional sense, we look upon our partnerships with others as mostly family, friends, co-workers and our "significant other." Today, Soqued Hozi, the "Angel of Partnership" reminds us that we are in partnership with every living, breathing organism on our planet and beyond. We are connected on many levels, and each and every connection bonds us with who we are as individuals. To think of it in these terms is rather "mind boggling." The following channeling session will put the "term" partnership into perspective.

Soqued Hozi And The "Joy Of Partnership"

It is with great delight that I bring all who reside on this earth plane and beyond together in a union of love. As the birds sing and the sun shines, so is your connection with God's entire universe. In great company, and never alone, each one of you must let go of the loneliness knowing that everything and everyone around you is your "guiding light." The separation is only in your mind. Your connection to your universe is only a "thought" away, and the comfort that you so yearn for is there at this very moment.

Know that you are worthy of this connection. Reach out and connect with everything you see. You are surrounded by a world full of love, and compassion if that's what you choose. Helping hands are everywhere, and to receive you only have to open your arms, as you claim the support and love that is all around you. Close the door to separation. Know that you hold a "special" place in the universe, and each connection that you make is a step towards your evolution. Keep an open heart and mind as you look for the goodness that is available at each moment. Partnership is a connection that can only be broken if you say so. Bless all of your relationships. Send love and light, and watch it return to you in ways you never imagined. Separation is a man-made misconception, and truly does not exist. Walk along your path with love, knowing that all of your many connections have taken you to where you are today. Blame will only slow you down. The light that you walk towards is your "ticket" to freedom. Allow the universe in all its glory to surround you. Bathe in the love and devotion. As the trees, birds, flowers, and sky surround you, know that you are precious and worthy of the partnerships that have opened their hearts to you. Learn and grow from each one. Bless them now, and move forward. The timing has never been better, so do not delay as your connections are but a gift among gifts. Look upon your day with thanks for all of the many partnerships that surround you in this very moment, for each one brings you the "special" lesson that will help your spirit to grow and flourish.

Shedding The Old Skin

There are times in all of our lives when we feel that we have come to a crossroads. I myself have had this happen on several occasions. We almost feel uncomfortable in our skin as if we are ready to "shed" the old and move forward. Although it can be an uncomfortable feeling, it is also quite exciting. I always seem to struggle with it because of the unknown. I often think to myself "What's the big deal? You've been through this before." For some reason, as human beings, we never really get used to the changes that are taking place. As I look over my life, these changes started at a very young age. Starting at age two, my life started to transform, and many of the people I clung to for security were taken away. For a young child, this can be devastating and very hard to understand. Adults can put this into perspective a lot easier than a young child, and yet somehow the universe feels confident that we can handle this. As I sit here this morning, I ask the angels to bring me some of their views on this subject. Here is what they had to say.

Channeling Raziel Who Brings Us His View On Knowledge

You are further than you think, my child. The horizon is bright and a turning point is close. Do not allow your apprehension to stop you from your transformation. This is but another step in your journey, and joy becomes the outcome. You are ready for this. It is time for your evolution to progress. Stop for but a moment and look back; bless the past as you move forward with joy in your heart. Your accomplishments have been many, and you will continue to learn and grow now at a much faster pace. This gift is once again yours, and you must put aside the old as you graciously welcome the new into your life.

I bless the past and choose to move forward in my life with joy and with ease! A great affirmation to use daily as you move forward on your path.

More Guidance Comes Through From The Angel Amarushaya

The energy multiplies, as many blessings are coming your way. Stand with your arms wide open now, as you lovingly accept the goodness that so yearns for your acceptance. We are pleased and excited for you. The waiting period is over, and all that is nurturing and special awaits you. Let go of all resistance. Release the old trauma of the past. It was but a lesson to get you where you are today. Thank your strong, and noble spirit for the work it has done. Your progression is to be admired, and a great celebration is at hand. You are free and must allow this wonderful energy to usher you to the next level of growth. Smile often. Smell the sweetness in the air. Watch as all of your hopes and dreams become a reality. The blessings that surround you are but a gift from the angelic realm, and we delight in presenting them to you.

Thank You, Sweet Angels

Angels, oh angels, stand by my side
Angels, oh angels, along for the ride
Watching for danger, keeping me safe
Knowing I trust them, always forever
With me they travel, every endeavor
Feeling their love, day after day
Devoted and loving, this is their way
Thank you, my angels, always a friend
Light shining down, healing to mend

Helping the people who ask for advice
Providing solutions always precise
Archangel Michael, guardian, friend
Raphael, Gabriel, Uriel too
Metatron, Ariel to name just a few

These are the angels who help us each day
Angels, oh angels, please show me the way
Teach me to laugh and how to cry, too
Angels, oh angels, oh how I love you

How our relationship grows through the years
Showing me kindness, wiping my tears
Embracing my spirit, so soft and so sweet
Guardian angel, you never retreat

Thank you, my angels, for standing by me
A gift from above who will set us all free
Allow me to learn from your kindness and love
A gift among gifts from God up above

Brown

Achievement

&

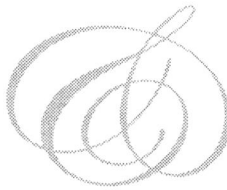

*Respecting
the World*

AUTUMN'S PURPOSE

It is the first day of autumn and my favorite time of year. The trees are starting to turn, and the weather is cool and crisp. What a wonderful time to pull back, and enjoy the warmth and the comfort that the season holds. As I watch the leaves turn color, I know that soon they will start to fall from the trees; it makes me think about the cycle of life. The earth has provided us with everything we need to move forward and allow change to occur.

Why is it that we as humans so often resist this change? Wouldn't it be much easier to shed the old and welcome the new as the seasons do? I also feel this is true with the people who play a role in our lives. Maybe it's the people we live with who make the biggest difference for us, or maybe it's our friends and co-workers. It may be a combination of all of the above. For family and friends are the foundations of our lives here on earth. Stop right now and think about the special people in your life. What role do they play? How do they affect us? Even the woman behind the counter at the market plays a role in our growth. Is it possible to shed the old beliefs about the people in our lives? Is it possible to start looking at them as shining lights, and opportunities for growth? Just as the trees here in the Northeast shed their old leaves, could it be time to dispel the old patterns and beliefs that have allowed the drama to play out for so long? What if we were to look at each person as if we had never met him or her before? Would this give us the opportunity to form a more spiritual opinion? We are given the opportunity to look at each fellow human being as friend or foe? It's really all a choice. Maybe it's time to look at those who bring us the biggest challenges as our "Special" Teachers. For in their messages there are great learning experiences. Allow the "chip" to fall from your shoulder, and be willing to look at the hidden lesson. It is there. If we put aside the "ego," our spirit will rise above, and the learning will take place.

As the trees go through the process of shedding their leaves in the fall, it is time for all of us as human beings to shed the old, as we bare our souls, and watch our rejuvenation process unfold. Just as the trees in the springtime bring forth the new crop of leaves so the process continues, as it does in each and every one of us here on the earth.

Autumn Leaves Must Fall

As I gaze from my window
The trees they do appear
The colors are so brilliant
So bright and so clear

The angels dance upon them
For fall is on the way
The weather it is crisp and cool
So watch and don't delay

For soon the trees will shed their coats
For all the world to see
They're not afraid to show the truth
For autumn it must be

A lesson for us all to learn
The truth it will prevail
A choice that we make every day
To sink to swim or sail
The trees go with the flow
As nature shows them how
To shed the old so newness reigns
So easy to allow

So, like a tree, I ask you
To shed your old skin, too

The flow will take you onward
Your life so fresh so new

Dispel the fear within you
Let love show you the way
The angels come to guide you
This choice you've made today

So now the spring will follow
Soul ready to renew
Your energies they flourish
Green grass and morning dew

So whether it's the colors of the
Autumn leaves so bright
Or winter's perfect snowflake
A holiday's delight

Springtime is for rebirthing
For all the world to see
Or the colors of the summer
The oceans flowing free

The season turns to autumn
Full circle it is clear
Another chance for cleansing
As our angels hold us near

Releasing Old Energies

I am reminded that even though I am an adult there are times when the "child" within me is still dealing with her old issues. As time passes, I see this in myself, as well as others, and often wonder "How can I move forward in my life?" and, in turn, help others to move forward, as well. Many of us have had some kind of old childhood trauma; whether it comes from our families or from outsiders really doesn't matter. It is the "beliefs" that we have adopted that become the true culprits in our lives. As adults, we feel that we should know better and that we should have it all under control. This may be true for the most part, but I have seen many episodes over the years where I have suffered needlessly with a great amount of upset and pain. The old patterns and trauma of my childhood have resurfaced many times, and I am no longer a fifty-one year old woman, but a five year old little girl who cries out for love and acceptance.

As I work with many of my clients, I can see that the child within them is in need of healing. I have had many bright and loving people sit in front of me feeling sad and forlorn because of childhood issues. At times like these I can see the "wounded" child, and know that I must somehow try to help them to heal.

Working with the angels has brought me a kind of "clarity" that I never experienced before. I have been able to look deeply at myself without judgment and with love in my heart. The process that I have been using came to me one morning, as I lay in bed thinking about my childhood experiences, wondering what it would have been like if as a child I knew what I know now. Think about that for a moment. What would that have been like for you? Maybe you would have been able to look at what was happening objectively, or maybe you would have had more of a choice about how you would have reacted to a particular person or situation. If you had known what you know now, you may have just walked away.

Through the many books and self-help seminars I have done over the years, one thing is certain, we are definitely spiritual beings having a human experience. I have been reminded of this many times in many different ways, and I would like to invite you now to look beyond what happened to you as a child, and start to allow the healing to take place. You and you alone will be able to make the difference. Self-love and appreciation are the keys. Not through a conceited or pompous attitude, but through knowing that each and every one of us is special, and that we all deserve the very best. If only we all believed this.

A very important issue was resolved this morning during my mediation with Jesus. As I brought his healing and rejuvenating white light through the top of my crown chakra, I could feel his warmth and love. I had been doing a lot of healing work with others, as well as myself, and felt that something was holding me back from my own healing. I was then instructed to do some EFT on the issue, and began the tapping process with the words "In Jesus' name I am healed." All of a sudden the word "worthy" was presented to me, and at that point I started to cry. This is unlike me since I usually don't cry that easily, and yet the emotion was deep, and the sadness overwhelming. It became crystal clear at that point that my healing wasn't manifesting because on some level I didn't feel "worthy." I had never really thought too much about this before. In most of my daily affirmations I use the word "deserving" or I would claim what I wanted to bring forth. I was then instructed to include the word "worthy" along with the rest of the tapping session, and, at the end of the process, I felt exhilarated and enlightened. The energy release that I had was one of great magnitude, and I realized that this one component was holding me back from truly enjoying and loving my life. As you read the process below, be willing to look deep within your own belief system, and make sure that you know that as a child of God you are truly worthy of everything that is good.

Healing The Wounded Child

First and foremost, you must start to adopt the belief that you are a worthy and lovable human being. This is a very important "key" to the healing process. As children, we were often taught that we were just "kids." This often brings about a feeling of not being good enough, or once again not feeling worthy.

In many religions we are taught over and over again to believe we are not worthy. As a child, I remember going to church and saying the words "Lord, I am not worthy to receive you, but only say the word and I shall be healed." This, to me, is a paradox. Repeating these words on a weekly basis truly fuels this belief, and over a period of time it becomes embedded in our subconscious mind. This, in itself, can be very limiting, and holds us back from what God truly wants for us. So the first step is to thank God for the gift of worthiness.

The next step is to apply this daily as a positive and supportive affirmation. For me this was a "true" awakening and brought about a great release from many of my life issues. Now, you are ready for the next step. I want you to find a picture of yourself; you know the one with that adorable little girl or boy, the one everyone loves. This, of course, is a picture of yourself that you really like. Now go out and buy a lovely frame for your picture, a frame that really feels like "you." Once you've put your child in his or her frame, it is time to find the "perfect" spot for your "little one." I have my child on my bureau across from my bed. As I wake up each morning, she is facing me. It's a great way to start the day. Now, you will want to put something pretty or meaningful around your picture. I have an angel and some flowers with several very positive affirmations surrounding my child. I have also put a "grown up" picture in a frame next to my child along with several healing crystals, rose quartz for love, and a crystal for clearing stagnant energies, along with an amethyst stone for healing and protection. What you decide to put is totally up to you.

Now that you have your altar all set, it's time to do the work. As you wake up each morning, you will sit up and face your child and adult. I like to say "good morning" and blow them each a kiss. Then, I tell them that they both deserve to have a happy, healthy and prosperous day. Next, I tell my child that she is important to me, and that I am here to support her throughout the day. I invite her to come to me with her needs and remind her that I am her most loving parent. I promise to listen and treat her with all the respect she deserves. This is a big part of the healing process. If you were to see this beautiful little girl or boy on the street, how would you treat them? You would probably smile, and think to yourself "what a beautiful little child." Now remember, this is you! As time goes by, you will start to get in touch more and more with the healing that needs to take place. Support and love this child like never before as you watch the transformation begin. Remember that children are very intuitive and creative, and that if we can get "in touch" with this part of ourselves, it becomes a well-deserved gift.

Allow this process to take place on a daily basis. Be committed to healing this beautiful soul that accompanied you to the earth plane. Your commitment will pay off, and you will begin to see that you are truly deserving of all the goodness that awaits you. I commend all who take on this process, for you are truly committed to having a rich and prosperous life.

Forever Free Process

You are in a comfortable and noise-free space. Now, take a few deep breaths and visualize yourself as a child. Scan your body for any sensations that may be coming up. Now, picture yourself being nurtured and loved by a parent or caretaker. Feel how wonderful their love can be. Now start to think of a situation with them that caused you pain or upset. It can be at any age. You are now standing in front of them, and God or one of your special angels is up above the two of you. As you look at your parent or person who has caused the pain, picture a cord running from them to you. It is time to do the "release" work. If you are truly committed to a life that is rich and full of prosperity, you are ready to begin. Think of the situation now and start to feel where it resonates in your body. Feel this sensation completely and be willing to go through it to the other side of the emotion. As you feel this emotion, you will cut the cord between you and the party that has caused the pain. As you cut the cord, you will fill your end with white light, and at the same time fill the other end that connects to them with the same healing light. Feel the joy and the release that takes place knowing that every cell of your body is beginning to heal. Use this process often and watch the release take place as your life becomes lighter and easier. You can also use this with everyday situations. The angels once again remind me that "forgiveness" is the way towards transformation and peace. So love with all your heart, and remember to forgive everyone including yourself!

Precious Child

A child dwells deep inside of me
A smile so warm, so sweet
A child dwells deep inside of me
Deep down inside retreat

The child is here now reaching out
For all the world to see
A bright and willing soul I feel
This child resides in me

A soft and tender voice I hear
Yet often times ignore
A tug that comes from deep within
The child now speaks once more

I am grown up, oh, this is true
Torn in so many ways
The hurts that I've encountered
Just wanting so to play

For deep inside is healing
So not to be afraid

It all unfolds so nicely
The healing for which you've prayed

For as God's child you're worthy
As worthy as can be
I truly now can see this
The truth that holds the key

A gift from God, this child we know
From heaven's pearly gates
Resides inside of all of us
For this is no mistake

So now I ask each one of you
To look down deep inside
The child within can heal us
Let go of fear and pride

Together we will follow
This path chosen from our birth
Together we will prosper
Our purpose here on earth

Again, I ask each one of you
To go within and see
The child that lies in all of us
A child who'll set us free

YOUR NOTES AND IDEAS

Champagne

Charity

Steps of Hope

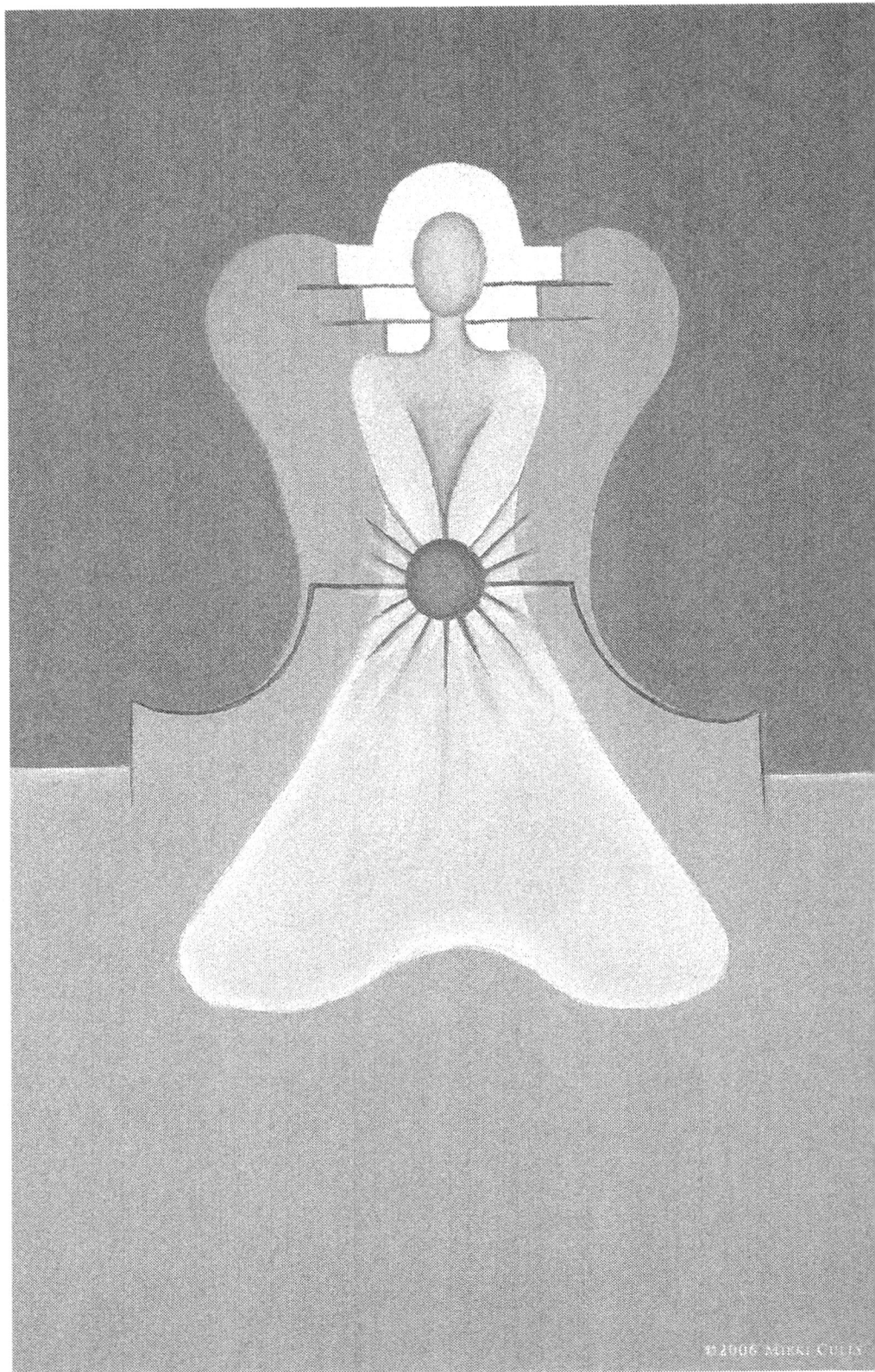

GIVING BACK

Because Americo Michael, Surrounded by Angels, is truly about transformation, it is my intention to bring this out into the world as a charitable and loving gift, not only to all who read the writings, but in donations to causes where I feel a true transformation can take place. One cause in particular is "The Garden of Angels" located in Yucaipa, California. Created in 1996 by Debi Faris-Cifelli, this wonderful heartfelt woman has brought hope and love to many abandoned children, as she spreads the word of support to new mothers who feel they have no where to turn. The Garden of Angels is both a sanctuary, and cemetery for abandoned children, and also a place where children can be helped to find homes as they are brought together with loving families. It is my hope that the donations from this book help to aid this process, and I invite any of you who are reading this to feel free to contact and donate to this wonderful organization. For what are we truly here on earth for but to love and support one another. For more information you can go to the website gardenofangels.org.

Monies will also be donated to:
The Katrina Restoration Fund, Oprah's Angel Network
Katrina Homes
P.O. Box 96600
Chicago, IL 60693

Jamie's Joy

Elene Bratton and Mychael McNeely established the Jamie's Joy Memorial Fund in loving memory of their five year old son Jamie who was taken from them in a car accident on April 24, 2002. The fund is to honor his beautiful spirit and the love and joy that their son brought to everyone in his life. The fund seeks to enrich the lives of all living beings by supporting activities, and organizations, that promote joy, love, connection and peace. These are the attributes that reflect the best of little Jamie. To learn more about Jamie's Joy, please visit www.jamiesjoy.org

Choosing Our Lives

As I continue to learn and grow here on earth, I realize that perfection is there for all of us. In each and every moment we have a choice. Whether we reach out to others or connect with source, the choice is ours. We can choose to pull back and retreat or move forward, holding our heads high, knowing that our future is bright. Intention plays a huge role in this. Remember whatever you concentrate on will eventually manifest in some way. I myself have had many obstacles to overcome in this lifetime. I have survived many losses, and have had to deal with many issues around fear and abandonment. Connecting with the angels and feeling their love and support, has been a true comfort to me, and such a gift from God. I happen to be one of those people who "feel" things very profoundly, and my emotions run not only high but deep. I have been likened to a "sponge" who can feel what others are feeling. At times it's hard to decipher my own feeling from others. My senses have always been extremely sharp, a great sense of smell, taste, hearing, and sight. I have learned much over the years through these gifts. I have also encountered health issues which at times were overwhelming, but one thing was always crystal clear; no matter what I had to go through, I was always being guided and helped by spirit. The term "The Universe Always Provides" is etched in my mind, and I have had many wonderful and supportive people by my side. I know now that all of my experiences have been for a purpose, and I know that each and every one of my physical and emotional experiences have made me a more understanding and loving human being. I have been told that I am the "wounded healer" and through my own search for answers, and my holistic approach, I have been able to heal myself and help others. This again is a gift. As we look at our lives, we can make the choice about how we look at the people, places, and situations that come to us each and everyday. A "curse" or a "gift," you decide.

Remember, whatever you give energy to will grow, so I suggest that you look at your life as a very special treasure, always remembering that growth will move you towards your divine purpose here on earth. My hope is that you have used the many channeling sessions, poems, healing techniques and stories to connect with yourself, loved ones who have passed, and the angels each and every day.

Phaneul helps me to end Americo Michael with his words of wisdom.

Channeling Phaneul Who Brings Us Hope

Do not feel lost for you are in good hands. There are so many energies supporting you at this time. The hope that surrounds both your spirit home and your earthly home are plentiful, and you are just where you need to be. Bless those who are leaving. Wish them well. They too are on their own journey, and it is time for them to move on. Do not hold on tight, for the energy will not flow this way. Your spirit is calm now, and all-knowing. Listen for it will guide you in the right direction. We must all make these changes so as not to live in "stagnant" waters. This is the cleansing that you have been waiting for. Put aside the fears that may come to you for this is just an illusion. Listen for our sweet voices and love and support from loved ones on the other side. Your army is plentiful and strong, so have trust and have faith in your decisions.

Deep within lie the answers to all of your many questions. Listen and watch as each one unfolds perfectly. Your new life is unfolding, and all you have to do is trust and accept that which is coming to you now with open arms.

Thank you, Phaneul, for your love and devotion.

As I end this book, I bless you all with the affirmations below.

If you like them and feel they could be useful in transforming your life, use them daily, for they are a gift from me to you. Each one starts with **"Through the grace of God."**

I am rich in consciousness and manifestation
I am well feeling full of energy and vitality
I am happy in my life, feeling joy and peace
I am healthy from head to toe
I am successful in my career and all of my relationships
I allow myself to receive all the goodness that comes my way
I am healed from all of the pain of the past
Through the grace of God "I am free" to live the authentic life that was truly meant for me to live

With Gratitude and Love to God, the Angels and Spirit,

Cathi Giannino Burke
Heavenly Messengers
heavenlymessengers.net

NAMASTE

The Angel Jamarerah comes through with Blessings

I am here to bring many blessings to Americo Michael "Surrounded by Angels." It is with great pleasure that I help you to manifest all that is good, as I help you to bring these divine writings out into the world. With all of the other Angels and Spirit I call forth all of the powers of Divine Prosperity, as I spread the word of Americo Michael. I am honored, and feel devoted to the writings which have been orchestrated for the good of all mankind. I am Jamarerah the Angel of Manifestation, and I am working with all of the Angels and Spirit in Americo Michael to bring peace, joy, love, healing, prosperity and harmony to all who choose to read the words and spread their love. As you begin to manifest your own goals and dreams I honor your wishes, and in the right time, and for your highest good these too will come to fruition. May Americo Michael "Surrounded by Angels" grow and prosper, and bring comfort and joy to all who have chosen to listen.

INDEX

Angels, Archangels & Goddesses

Affirmations

Angel signs

Healing Angel Pictures along with their colors & meanings

The Healing "Chakra" Angels & their Colors

Red	Ariel
Orange	Archangel Michael
Yellow	Daniel and Sarah
Emerald Green	Cassiel
Light Blue	Celestina and Faith
Indigo	Archangel Gabriel
Violet	Archangel Raphael

Poems by Cathi Giannino Burke

Processes

CPSIA information can be obtained at www.ICGtesting.com
Printed in the USA
BVOW08s0746260815

415070BV00001B/5/P